RÉSUMÉ SUCCESS!

INSIDER SECRETS TO BUILDING THE RÉSUMÉ TOP COMPANIES LOVE!

DAVID J. GARDNER

The Great Success Club Publishing

The Great Success Club Publishing
Résumé Success! Inside Secrets to Building the Résumé Top Companies LOVE!

Unattributed quotations are by David J. Gardner

Edition ISBNs
Soft cover   978-0-9864742-0-0
Ebook   978-0-9864742-1-7
Audiobook   978-0-9864742-2-4
DVD Audiobook   978-0-9864742-3-1

For more information about the products, services, and presentations offered by David J. Gardner, visit the website www.davidjgardner.com

The Great Success Club and logo are the property of David J. Gardner
Printed in the United States of America and Canada

RÉSUMÉ
SUCCESS!

For Kumiko, Logan, and William.
You strengthen me every day.

To the Gardner, Tomimatsu, Sherman, Miles,
and MacMillan clans...I'm so lucky to have you!

Acknowledgements

There are so many people who helped me, directly or otherwise, bring this book into reality.

Thank you so very, very much:

- ✧ Kumi and the boys, who supported me so resolutely through it all.
- ✧ Mum, for only wanting what's best for me always, I love you.
- ✧ My dear sisters Paula and Nina, for remaining close and caring always.
- ✧ Miyuki, for all your help through so much of this you're wonderful; Nobuaki, for being a great uncle to the boys.
- ✧ Hisashi and Minako, for welcoming me into your family and supporting our life.
- ✧ Steve and Firth, for keeping the gals so very happy.
- ✧ Sue, Don, Chris, Don, Phil, Sheilaugh, and kids…for being such a great extended family.
- ✧ Diane, for being there.
- ✧ Barrie, for being a true brother and your close friendship for over 25 years.
- ✧ Thanks to Rick Soldin, for guiding the design to greatness (http://book-comp.com)
- ✧ Thank you Dan Poynter for guiding me through the process, and responding so quickly when I needed it most.

The Résumé Success Insider 600

The more than 600 years of recruitment experience that went into the research for this book comes almost equally from great agency and corporate recruiters.

Many, many thanks to the following **agency recruiters** for your input:

Rakesh Kothary, Paul Farkas, Neil Kouba, Tom Rainey, Janet Chappell, Shireen Dietrich, Alicia Kalozdi-MacMillan, Trish O'Quinn, Carla Perry, Danny Dipaolo, David Jerrett, Brian Drake, Nadine Huckvale, Jeff Aplin, Jacqueline Gallagher, Laurie

Stirling, Greg Ford, Laura Paton, Sean Armstrong, John Perry, Gary Van Donkersgoed, Nikki Palmer, Jacqui Lesperance, Ben Tipping, Chris Kershaw, and Nicole Bradfield, currently working at levels from consultant to partner in over 15 different agencies.

The following **corporate recruiters** also lent their vast wisdom and knowledge working for top companies in North America to the Insider 600 group. Thank you!

Reeshma Jassani, Peter Shenfield, Cheryl Malton, Dee Sharma, Elise Graziano, Cindy Isaak, Mary Jackson, Sarah Chapman, Pam Mihailoff, Martin Choquette, Maxine Clarke, Cheryl Deneau, Willie French, Georgina Mouratidis, Maurice Fernandes, Melissa Hoover, Sumbo Ashabo, Ian Caldwell, Meldon Wolfgang, Patti Clarkson, Carla Spadafora, Peter Ciccia, Patti Cross, Maya Toussaint, Louise Saint-Pierre, Brenda Brown, Cheryl Malton, Anita Sampson Binder, Regina Ramos, Kim Vu, Jennifer Knight, Anya Mikhailyuk, Leslie Lodewyk, Nelson Chan, Matt Bateman, Salome Chopra, Sandi Nielsen, Natasha Gill

Corporate recruiters represented these **top North American companies** (parentheses indicates where they sit on the US or Canadian *'Top 100 Companies to Work For'* List from *Fortune* and *MacLeans* magazines). Canadian companies were not rated numerically.

NetApp (#1 US)
CGA Canada (Top 100 Canada)
Ceridian (Top 100 Canada)
The Boston Consulting Group (#3 US)
Blake, Cassels & Graydon LLP
Pivotal Solutions (Top 100 Canada)
EPCOR (Top 100 Canada)
Chatham Kent Health Alliance (Top 100 Canada)
The Methodist Hospital System (#8 US)
Smuckers (US/Cdn Confectionary)
Canadian Pacific (Top 100 Canada)
Enbridge (Top 100 Canada)
Fairmont Hotels and Resorts (Top 100 Canada)
Yellow Pages Group (Top 100 Canada)
Paychex (#39 US)
Compass Group Canada (Top 100 Canada)
Carswell (Thomson Reuters)
Alberta-Pacific Forest Industries Inc. (Top 100 Canada)
Rogers Communications (Top 3 Telecom Canada)
Medigas (Praxair)
Canada Bread (Maple Leaf Foods)
Bayer (Top 100 Canada)

Many thanks also to the numerous individual recruiters and organizations that contributed to the research but chose to remain unlisted here.

Contents

Do not underestimate the power of a great résumé! It has the power to open doors or slam them shut. This is your first impression, and possibly your only chance to score an interview... make the most of it!

Cindy Isaak—Recruiter
Paychex, USA

chapter 1

The Beginning Bits

Welcome…and congratulations! By picking up this book you've begun a journey far too few people hoping to land that next great job embark upon:

The journey to a successful résumé.

A knock em' dead, top 5% in your field, enjoyable to read, convincing, honest, earnest, balanced, incredibly powerful résumé.

Surprisingly, over 90% of job hunters don't take the time or effort to read a quality book or consult a genuine expert on résumé creation. Instead, they feel contented to download a template, revamp their own old résumé, borrow a résumé from a colleague or peer and model it, or just do the best they can based upon what they believe is correct.

The results usually speak for themselves, as these same people wait anxiously for the call to interview that never comes. It's depressing. The silent phone and empty email inbox force them to loosen their expectations (and integrity) and send out vast quantities of résumés to companies that are less appealing and less a match for their skills…and often farther from home or at lower pay. If they ultimately accept one of these lesser positions they are less likely to enjoy it, thrive, and stay long term. And so they begin what should be a great next step in their professional career with one eye already on the door.

It's a sad cycle, and unnecessary.

Whether the economy is shrinking or expanding, there will **always** be a need for strong talent in virtually every field. If you are good at what you do, it's just a matter of helping a great company understand how great **you** are to get that interview, and then, that fantastic job.

The *résumé* will do this.

The purpose of this book is to help you create the strongest résumé in your marketplace as quickly, easily, and thoroughly as possible.

The résumé is the most important marketing document a person will ever create.
Maurice Fernandes— Recruitment Manager, Ceridian

Why You Need a New Résumé

Over 98% of professional-level jobs posted by companies in North America require that you submit an up-to-date résumé. As Internet job boards make the hiring world smaller and the availability of new jobs open to almost anyone with a computer connection, the competition for any one role has drastically increased. Depending upon the particular job, your résumé will likely be measured against between 60–120 others…sometimes more or less, depending on your market and location, and **only the top 10 or less will be contacted for that one job.**

You need a new résumé because more and more positions demand it as an absolute requirement, and competition is intense.

Less than 50 years ago, you could expect to work for one employer your whole life. You sign up with a company or firm straight out of university or college, or even high school, and toil away until you retire and earn that golden watch. For good or ill, the days of the one job until you retire are long gone. In fact, it's now estimated that the average North American will change jobs every 3–4 years, and according to the U.S. Department of Labor, a person will change **entire careers** 3–5 times in their life!

You need a new résumé because you will change your jobs every few years and each new one will demand it.

You will learn in this book that there are some ingredients in a great résumé that are both universal and long-standing. Many more, however, are reflections of newer technology and increased skill and efficiency by recruiters to help them deal with the abundance of job seekers. Being technology and trend-based, these latter examples mean that in order to be competitive, your résumé must always reflect these most recent expectations and innovations. If your résumé is more than a few years old it will stick out like the fossil it has become.

You need a new résumé because your last résumé is already obsolete.

I Understand

If I were to ask you to write down your **Top 50 Most Enjoyable Things To Do** I can pretty well guarantee that writing a résumé wouldn't be on that list. Or your top 50,000 list for that matter! In fact, creating a résumé ranks right up there with cleaning the garage…after a flood…in the dark.

But it must be done. Not only must it be done, it must be done so well that you stand out amongst the countless people who will be competing in the same industry you are. It must be done, or you will **not even have the chance** to interview for that next job.

This book will give you everything you need to build the ultimate résumé as easily as possible. In the following pages you will not only learn how to create a successful résumé, but you will gain a number of peripheral skills and perspectives that will help you long term as you progress in your profession.

You will also develop the ability to create your future résumés quickly and with greater potency than your peers. People will compliment your résumé, you will get more interviews, more offers, and be hired quickly at better companies, in better roles, and with better pay.

By providing this step-by-step guide I hope to raise the image of the maligned résumé if not to the level of respect it deserves…at least to the point that it may crack your **Top 50,000 Most Enjoyable Things To Do** list…maybe. It takes some time and effort but, armed with the right information, creating a résumé to position a job-hunter in the top 5% in their field is a lot easier than most people think.

And you will build one that's *great*. I promise.

| INSIDER SECRET | Recruiters are busy. The tool they use to immediately weed out over 90% of applicants is the **résumé.** If it's not great, it's garbage. |

Why Is This Book Not Bigger?

This book could have easily been made several times longer. In fact, many of the books I read in my research were well over 450 pages, packed with generalities, personal opinion, and situations rarely applicable in real life. The initial draft of this book was swelling to an ultimate 350+ pages before I realized that **I would never read a whole book that thick on résumés** myself! Instead I would just skim for important bits that apply to my situation. I would want results and want them as quickly as possible. My time is too valuable to be wasted and I assume the same is true for you.

When I came to that conclusion I knew that this book must be concise. It must include everything it needs without a single page more. It cannot under any circumstances go over 300 pages, I resolved. Creating the ultimate résumé does **not,** I had learned, require a tome the size of *War and Peace.*

I designed this book to be much like a résumé: succinct, clear, powerful, and as brief as possible while providing all the vital information. If a section has been included here, even if it may seem less relevant than others, it has been added to provide you the perspective necessary to get the most out of the whole process.

Where Are You Now?

You may be unemployed now and looking for the edge to get you ahead of other job seekers in your marketplace. You may be employed in a role that you're not happy with and feel the need to 'see what's out there'. You may be fresh out of school or new to the country and are hoping to get that foot in the door. Perhaps you have an old résumé you're trying to make current and relevant, or perhaps you've never built one before, and are nervous about the prospect.

Whether you are applying for a $25,000 position as a data entry clerk, or a $2.5M CEO, this book will not discriminate level, profession, or work history. The experience and research that came together to create this book have proven that an extremely well designed résumé following the strategies outlined will perform equally well at every salary level in virtually every field.

What got you here and how much you have earned in the past doesn't matter. The road to a successful next career move begins with an excellent résumé. Not average, not okay, not good, but **excellent.** Anything less places you down among the myriad other hopefuls, and you just don't need to be there.

As in life, your résumé should be ever changing and evolving— keep it current!
Sandi Nielson— Recruitment Consultant, Alberta-Pacific Forest Industries Canada

Tech-Savvy?

I credit the reader with enough technical savvy to understand the basics of word processing and use of the Internet. I'll not waste time and space instructing you how to open a Word document and change a font since the majority of readers will be comfortable with it to the degree they will have no issues. I will simply show you fonts and tell you which of them are best to use and why.

The good news is that one needs only fundamental computer skill to create a world-class résumé, and then to get it into the right hands. Whether you are an Internet noob, born of the hunt-and-peck keyboarding school, or a techno uber-whiz, the process will remain the same and the product will be equally impressive.

Wherever possible I will avoid using reference to an online website. The Internet is changing so rapidly that by the time this book is six months old some links may be dead as the technology and information move on. During my research I encountered countless defunct references online, and it's just plain frustrating. The strategies themselves are more relevant and timeless and so I will avoid relying upon currently popular e-links.

Homework

There will be exercises for you to complete...please do them! If you are in a management-level or executive position you may feel that you have the basics down and can skim over some information and get to the 'meat' of this book. Avoid the temptation! You will learn that there are just **five** key areas you need to master in order to have an unstoppable résumé and we will work through them systematically. These five, called **The 5 Master Keys to Résumé Success,** will be explained in detail as we work together to create your ultimate professional document.

If you are asked to brainstorm, consider an option, list, or do some research, it is a powerful and necessary task. Chapters contain specifically ordered steps to carry you through the process and ignoring any one of them may result in a less-than-fantastic résumé. Read every word, follow methodically, and have a highlighter and notebook handy; it'll be worth it. I have included a chapter synopsis at the end of each section, so please review these to ensure that you have not missed something important.

What This Book Is Not

This book is not designed to help you choose what you want to be when you grow up! It is assumed that you have at least an idea of your overall direction. You really do need to have an awareness of your field and possible next steps before you read on. If you haven't a clue what to do with your career, there are some outstanding career choice books out there you should begin with. *What Color is your Parachute,* by Richard Nelson Boles, reprinted every year since 1970, remains an outstanding starting point for people looking for their calling...or **next** calling. Go there first. Following that, please come back to this book and you will create a dynamite résumé to move you to that career goal.

The Real Value of a Résumé

In order to truly appreciate the importance of an excellent résumé, it's worthwhile to consider its value...so how much is your résumé worth?

If the average length of time we stay at one job is 3–4 years (actually less than this now, but let's make this a conservative estimate), and the average North American annual income is approximately $45,000 (based on Statistics Canada and US Labor Relations data 2008–2009), then the average job is worth about $180,000 in total. Make sense so far? Now you may make more or less than this, but if so, simply multiply your income per year by 4 and you have the total worth of that job averaged versus present day norms.

Now, in order to get this $180,000 job, you must pass through two vital stages. Firstly, you must have a résumé so strong that you make the recruiter's short list (usually 3–9% of applicants, with the average at 6%). Secondly, you must interview well enough to land the job.

You will NOT get the chance to interview unless your résumé is in that top group!

Since the résumé is the first, mandatory step towards hire, and since only the top résumés submitted have a chance of being contacted, it can be readily argued that your résumé is worth $180,000! If yours is **not** good enough, you must understand, you will not be contacted and that $180,000 job goes to someone else.

Even if you disagree with this oversimplification of fact, at the very least the difference between an excellent résumé and an average one has a significant imputed value. Salary, length of job search, quality of company found, work/life balance, opportunities for growth, all of these have real money worth to you. Your top choice company may offer the perfect mix. But without a top résumé you won't get a chance to work at that company, or even your second-tier choice, or tenth. How much money is a great job worth to you? Thousands of dollars? Absolutely...and then some! A great résumé gets you hired earlier, to a better employer, with more money, flexibility, and options for the future.

I'm pretty easy to please when it comes to résumés... which is all the more reason to be surprised that I see SO few good ones!

Nicole Bradfield— Recruitment Consultant, Placement Group

The Résumé Gatekeeper

Some might argue that it's the experience that gets you the interview and ultimately the job. This is not necessarily so! Experience history that suits the role is very important, but relevant experience can easily be trumped by résumé and interview ability! I have seen hundreds of outstanding applicants with very strong, relevant experience passed by due to a poor résumé.

When you submit your résumé to a company, the first person to review it will likely not be the hiring manager. Instead, a recruiter or Human Resources employee I call the 'Résumé Gatekeeper', is your résumé's first stop. If they don't like it, it goes no further. If the Résumé Gatekeeper isn't impressed then there are **always** other candidates to consider. Through the course of this book I will use the terms Résumé Gatekeeper and recruiter interchangeably. However named, they represent the first vital destination for your résumé.

Your résumé is going to 'speak' to a recruiter before you get a chance to. Make sure that it speaks well of you, and continually revise and update.
Willie French—Director, Talent Acquisition, Methodist Hospital System, USA

Résumés: Art or Science?

Some résumé books go on at length about the 'art' of their creation, how elusive perfection is and how finding the right ingredients can be challenging. They rely upon tricks and gimmicks to spark reader attention and to get them into the right hands. Some use audacious bright colors and funky fonts, innovative submission strategies and chocolate bribes. Others reviewed were more subtle, with graphs, charts, personal watermarks, personal online résumés, and boastful content. These résumés, they argued, were original, noticeable, and therefore would increase the applicant's chances to get a call.

Nonsense!

Creating a fantastic résumé is not some strange alchemy, and you will not need to resort to amateur attention-grabbing tactics to be seen. The way to the ultimate résumé is much more a science than an art! There exist rules you will learn and principles you will follow that will make your skills, experience, and professional self far more attractive and compelling than your peers.

> The incredible irony is that due to the real fact that there are so *few* truly well designed and powerfully created résumés in circulation; yours *will* be startlingly different as it will be a welcomed rarity in recruiters' eyes.

INSIDER SECRET

A Little History

I was much like anyone before I became a professional agency recruiter, reviewing countless résumés each week. I knew résumés were important but had no idea **how** important or that the slightest change could be the difference between being called for interview or ending up in the trash bin. I had little interest in and knowledge about making my own résumé from scratch.

Everything changed once I became a recruiter. Tens, hundreds, thousands of résumés would hit my inbox and I would review and evaluate them all, deciding what small percentage would get an interview with me. I learned innumerable lessons in visual appeal, content, organization, and strategy that would impress me or turn me off.

I began to realize the real power of a résumé. If it was great, I would meet the person…if it was poor, I wouldn't. It was that simple. And If I didn't meet them, then my colleagues wouldn't, and the companies I was recruiting for wouldn't.

> **An interview and job or nothing all based on the strength of one brief document…**

Wanting to Help

As time went by it became easier and easier to tell the differences in résumé quality. I naturally began to classify résumés into levels: poor, fair, good, and excellent. Unfortunately, while **only an excellent résumé would guarantee an interview with me,** the majority of fair or even many good résumés would be filed away and perhaps never touched again. With just enough quality applicants with an excellent résumé it was an easy cut to make. The majority of them were unremarkable and therefore unqualified...and still more were awkward and poorly organized. My heart went out to the unsuccessful applicants. Why didn't they get it? Who taught them how to create such unappealing résumés?

When I forced myself to thoroughly search through the chaos of even a mediocre résumé I often saw kernels of potential. Some of these people **could** be great new hires for my clients! But unless they completely overhauled their résumés, **no one** would meet them.

It became common practice for me in my interviews to help people improve their résumés. I would give them feedback and assign them 'homework' to fix areas I knew weren't good enough. Those who followed through interviewed more often than their underequipped peers, and got job offers more quickly and in greater number. Oddly enough, some did **not** take my advice, given freely, and continued to spin their wheels and wonder why no one wanted to hire...or even interview them. These people ultimately decided that volume would do what quality would not, and they spammed out countless copies of their lackluster résumé to anonymous web portals. I couldn't help though, because their résumé just wasn't good enough to send on to the companies I was recruiting for and now it had become a dime-a-dozen commodity.

I began to work on a report detailing how to make a better résumé. I thought that if I wrote down everything I know about what makes a résumé successful, I could send it to anyone who asked and help improve their ability to land their next job. Before I finished, however, I realized that although the guide I was making would reflect the views of many recruiters and companies, I couldn't be sure that I was truly the best authority on the subject. In the end it would simply be **my** opinion.

I decided to discover what the overwhelming consensus of recruiters, separated from their own personal opinions and preferences, consistently love to see in a résumé.

The Résumé Success 600 Years Insider Team Survey

I turned to a group of skilled and successful agency recruiters to find out what they thought made a perfect résumé. I designed a survey posing a list of questions to drill down to the essential, nitty-gritty details of what worked and didn't work, what caught their interest or turned them off. My aim was to have over 250 years worth of great recruiter input from more than 20 agency backgrounds.

As the results came in I was surprised at how powerful the collected statistics were. If every person who sent us their résumé had this information and used it, we would feel compelled to meet all of them!

I went to the library and took out several books on résumé creation. I went to bookstores, talked to staff about the most recent and popular books, and bought the most popular seven to review. I was blown away to discover that most of these books were far off the mark in guessing what recruiters really want! Some were good, but they didn't go far enough. Some were poor, and tried to package their opinions with flashy banners and high page counts. Many were jammed with obsolete information.

Not one of them seemed to have the *full* picture.

Part of the reason stemmed from the fact that they were largely the opinion of one person. Perhaps the author had been fixing résumés for years, or in some instances been a recruiter at a large company for their entire career. Some fine experience, but all from **one** perspective, and very subjective!

Another reason for the feeling of disconnect was that many of them approached the issue from the job-seeker side of the table. How wrong! The answer to what makes a great résumé has to come from the **recruiter** side! **Our** perspective as recruiters is the only one that matters, since our opinions are the ones that open or shut the door on your application.

> You must approach the creation of your résumé understanding that it is the *recruiter's* opinions, loves, peeves, biases, and priorities that matter, and not your own.

INSIDER SECRET

More than this, as I pored over the results of my survey and compared it to my own conclusions, I found striking similarities, patterns that could be made into rules for all to follow. I had realized that there was a science to the perfect résumé…a formula I could learn and teach others…and no one seemed to have understood that yet.

It was that day I decided I had to write this book.

But even then I didn't think my research was deep enough. Not yet. Agency recruiters can be highly skilled and must cater to the résumé desires of multiple client companies with multiple demands. But what about the hiring companies themselves? What did **their** recruiters love in a résumé? I needed to extend my research to include that end-user, the very companies my candidates want to join.

The Top Companies to Work For

Every year, *Fortune* magazine in the US, and *MacLean's* magazine in Canada put out a list of the **'Top 100 Companies to Work For'.** I went to a representative number of these companies with a newer, updated electronic survey designed to discover what for them makes a résumé great. The survey contained more than thirty multiple choice, short, and long answer questions.

I certainly could have approached **'Fortune 500'** companies at first glance they might seem the best place to go; they **are** corporate powerhouses, after all. But this book is for **you,** the applicant, the job searcher, and you want to work for a company that takes care of its people. The Fortune 500 list consists of the U.S. companies with the highest gross revenue that year. An outstanding achievement, **but inclusion on that list doesn't automatically make it a great place to work.**

You could work for a **'Fortune 10'** company for that matter and suffer such anxiety and stress that you wished you were elsewhere. Nowadays people want balance, to work hard in a great environment, with strong benefits, a sense of community conscience, loyalty, opportunity for growth, and a brand name to be proud of. The list of 'Top Companies to Work For' provides that. You will also find input from some other top companies in brand-name recognition and strong history, such as

Smuckers. Their input is similarly valuable. Some companies agreed proudly to have their names published here, and others contributed but asked for anonymity (they felt they were letting out their résumé selection secrets), which I respected.

And don't worry. If you want to work for a Fortune 500 company the information in this book will get you there, too. As it turns out some of the 'Top Companies to Work For' are **also** Fortune 500 companies.

The research wasn't easy. Recruiters at top companies are harried, and very guarded with their time. They don't tell the general public what they like to see in résumés because not only are they are busy, but also **it's not their job to do so!** As a writer, though, I gained access to this insider group and had the opportunity to ask them what they really loved in some résumés…and what made them toss the rest in the garbage.

The end results provided me over 300 years of résumé reviewer input from top companies. The total combined set of agency and corporate recruiters totaled over 600 years! Comparing the results I found similarities and differences that led to a further refinement of my formula…and now I had the research to back it up. I called our group, this potent team of top present-day recruitment professionals the **'Résumé Success 600 Years Insider Team'**, or **'Résumé Success 600'** for short.

All the Industries and All the Areas

Companies surveyed span an impressive range of top industries such as: Healthcare, Industrial, Manufacturing, Utilities, Hospitality, Services, Technology, Natural Resources, Transportation, Pharmaceuticals, Food, Aerospace, Telecommunications, Consulting, Confectionary, and Recruiting.

Contributions came from recruiters in the United States, Canada, and the UK, with over 310 years of corporate recruiting experience and 290 years of agency recruiter experience, totaling over 600 years of current recruiting wisdom.

The **Résumé Success 600** routinely recruits for professionals in these areas: Accounting, Human Resources, Information Technology, Sales, Engineering, Supply Chain, Office Personnel, General Labor, Marketing,

Finance, Legal, Technical/Professional, Hospital/Healthcare—RN's, RPN's all hospital roles except Physicians, General Medical, Operations, Consulting, Railway Specific Positions, Temporary, Regulatory and Safety Coordinators, Spa, Graphic Design, Communication, Food service, Hospitality, Skilled Trades, Executives, Semi-skilled Foreign Workers, Facility Management, Housekeeping, Foresters, and more.

This brain trust of professionals from both sides of the recruiting field receive an average of 15,035 résumés each week. That means collectively we evaluate **every year** over 781,820 résumés! Combining the average résumés received daily with the number of years experience, this incredible group of recruiters bring to you the wisdom of evaluating over a staggering **7.2 MILLION RÉSUMÉS!!!!**

I found that it didn't matter in which industry a recruiter worked, there was a surprising universality in the specifics they expected from a successful résumé. Some aspects consistently made their top lists of 'love to see' or 'hate to see' regardless of industry background. Some made good common sense and others shocked me in their counter-intuitiveness.

I have included a wealth of **Quotes, Insider Secrets,** and **Survey Highlights** throughout this book to give you unique insight into the thoughts, beliefs, standards, and opinions of the real-life recruiters who professionally review résumés like yours every day.

The 5 MASTER KEYS to Résumé Success

As mentioned earlier, despite the sheer volume and variety of research I had compiled, discernable patterns began to form. Before long, five distinct areas of the résumé process again and again surfaced as being vital for total résumé success.

It didn't matter if applicants were sales professionals or accountants, young or old, men or women, people who got their résumé to me and ended up in that select 5% I call and interview had mastered certain areas relating to their résumé. When a candidate did not know enough to master at least one of these areas their chance of having an interview was 0%. I never met them. If they had become skilled in at least one area, they had a chance to meet me, but it remained slim. But when they had all five areas mastered, I would **always** meet them.

It was a virtual interview guarantee!

Every single aspect of a great résumé falls into one of these categories. Sure enough, as results of the surveys from both agency and corporate recruiters came in, their responses echoed my own discovery.

The 5 Master Keys to Résumé Success:

- Knowledge

- Experience

- Format

- Content

- Submission

Let's take a moment to better understand each area and what it contributes to résumé excellence, and the sort of topics we will cover.

KNOWLEDGE refers to having a sound understanding of what a résumé is, the hiring process companies use, the most current trends in résumé application, and so on. If you don't have a strong foundational grasp of these things, you are likely going to make the same fatal résumé mistakes most people do. You won't understand the what, where, when, how, and why of résumé creation. You must educate yourself and really understand what a résumé is, or risk making a document that has no impact on a recruiter. Here are some examples of questions easily answered by those who master the Knowledge Key:

- Even a poor résumé will get you an interview if your experience is strong, right?

- An online service advertises that it will build your résumé for $20, what do you do?

- An agency recruiter at a busy, successful firm says she will work with you but you must agree to work **only** with her…is she on your side or not?

- What's the difference between a good and a great résumé?

- A friend of yours is an Internet whiz and tells you that he can get your résumé posted on every major posting board and site in your area. Do you take him up on it?

- Should you have a résumé, even if you're working?
- Is there a standard that recruiters use to evaluate résumés, or is it completely arbitrary?

Armed with a strong understanding of what a résumé really is, what it needs to do, the most valuable sections, the players involved, and everything else within this book will lead to your being able to answer these questions and make important decisions on the fly to vastly increase your chances of that interview and job offer.

EXPERIENCE deals with everything you bring to the table in your employment history. You may believe that a résumé is simply a listing of your prior professional roles, but so what? Every position, regardless of how junior or senior it may be requires an employee to perform a lengthy list of responsibilities, some of which may change frequently...so which do you list on your résumé? Some common questions surrounding Experience follow:

- Which responsibilities are most relevant on your résumé?
- If you had multiple titles, which do you list?
- If you were very good at a part of your job, how do you let a recruiter know it?
- Which specific parts of your experience do recruiters want to know about?
- Are there areas of your experience you should hide?
- How far into the past should you go?
- What if you have no employment experience?
- What information should you list about the companies themselves?

The way you detail your history can help convince a recruiter not only that their role is the best next step for you in your career, but also that your development makes you a perfect fit for their position and culture.

Experience is the raw material with which you build a great résumé. Imagine your overall experiences, responsibilities, and contributions as a vast forest...which trees are the right ones to build with? Choosing poorly will result in a weakly built résumé, but the best experiences, organized well will stand strong against recruiter scrutiny and peer competition.

FORMAT is the structure of your résumé, its layout. Before a recruiter reads a single word, the structure of your résumé alone can attract or repel, demonstrate confidence or uncertainty. Spacing, style, fonts, number of pages, these are all aspects of résumé structure. Recruiters have certain expectations as to how a great résumé is laid out. If you do it well, they will be surprisingly receptive to the content. You will discover in Format answers to such questions as these:

- How many pages are ideal for a résumé?

- There are many different formats, which is right for you?

- What is white space and is it important?

- Is there one style of font that outperforms others?

- What sections should you include? Does it really make a difference?

- Is there a layout that recruiters like most?

- What do you do when your résumé is too long…or too short?

In the first 5 seconds a recruiter screens your résumé, format is the most important factor in determining if you remain on her screen for consideration, or are saved into her system but deleted from her screen…and mind.

CONTENT refers to the carefully chosen words in your résumé; fleshing out everything you represent professionally and making you shine. Grammar, syntax, spelling, tense, register, these are all aspects of Content, and the words chosen make a tremendous difference to your appeal as an applicant.

- When, where, if ever should you use full sentences in your résumé?

- What words make the difference on a résumé? Where do you use them?

- Does spelling really matter? How much?

- Past, present, future…which tense is right on a résumé?

Keep it short, chronological, and meaningful. Clear and concise is the mantra! Show us what you've done… you've accomplished. We don't want to know what you would do, as we'd all be heroes in our own minds!
Anita Sampson-Binder—Director of Recruiting, Compass Group

- Do bullet lists help or hurt your chances?

- Do adjectives make your résumé stronger? If not, what works?

SUBMISSION is the final of **The 5 Master Keys to Résumé Success,** concerned with getting your résumé into the right hands at the right time. A poorly submitted résumé may not reach the relevant recruiter, or may be perceived as spam. Duplicating your submission efforts can disqualify your résumé entirely. The following questions represent the kinds of challenges that this area can provide:

- How do you submit your résumé to give you the best chance of an interview?

- The more résumés you send out the better, right?

- Who at a company is it best to send your résumé to?

- Should you follow up? If so, when and how often?

- When you send your résumé, where exactly does it go?

- How long after you send in your résumé should you call to check if they got it? Should you call at all?

- How many companies should you send your résumé to at once? How do you choose which ones?

- What about agency recruiters?

- Are job fairs a waste of time?

- How should you organize your job search efforts?

If you master the Submission area, you will always know where it is and that it's being actively considered by the best person. Our research indicates that up to 40% of all résumé submissions are ignored due to simple mistakes the applicant makes in the process that turns off a recruiter.

In the following chapters we will cover each of the 5 Master Key areas, and master them you will! Also included are chapters on putting the keys together called Let's Build it and Cover Letter, which deserve special mention in order to bring your new résumé to the level of great success you desire.

Now let's get started!

Chapter 1 Summary

- You need a new, powerful résumé due to:
    - Its necessity by employers
    - Fierce competition
    - The frequency of job/role/career changes you face
    - The obsolete nature of your current résumé
- This book is designed to make a résumé in the top 5% in virtually any field as simply and clearly as possible
- It doesn't take a 500 page book to help create a top tier résumé
- This book provides a step-by-step process, and every task given is important
- This book will not help you decide what you want to be, but having decided, presents the most recent, relevant, powerful insider information to get you that next job
- A résumé is the most important professional document of your career; without it you will **not** get an interview or job
- The Résumé Gatekeeper is the first and most important recipient of your résumé; you must impress them or your résumé goes no further
- There is a formula to the ideal résumé
- This book contains over 600 years of recruitment wisdom from both agency and corporate recruiters in top companies Canada and the USA with experience from entry level to executive applicants in over 20 varied fields
- **The 5 Master Keys to Résumé Success:**
    - Knowledge
    - Experience
    - Format
    - Content
    - Submission

A successful job search is more than being able to recite your résumé, you must truly understand what your audience is looking for and then be able to outline your objectives and expectations to either the interviewer or your recruiter. If you don't do your homework, your job search may be doomed.

Rakesh Kothary
—Sr. Search Consultant,
Mason Group Recruiting

chapter 2

Master Key #1: KNOWLEDGE

Knowledge is power, but only if you know how best to **apply** it. Understanding the real purpose of a résumé, the hiring process, recruitment, and identifying what role and type of company is most compatible for you will set you far apart from your marketplace competition. You will easily navigate the often-intimidating waters of the job hunter. You will have a peace of mind that others in your field searching for their next job will not share. Not only will it lead you to build a stronger résumé, you will make improved decisions, position yourself more adeptly in your market, identify better opportunities, and progress quickly in whatever business direction you choose to take.

In short, you will have the power to do much more than someone with a similar professional pedigree. That is the power of Knowledge, the first Master Key.

You Don't Know What You Don't Know About Résumés…Yet!

Educating yourself before, during, and following the résumé creation process will help you develop a kind of professional acuity from which you will draw both conscious and non-conscious benefits going forward.

The **Four Stages of Learning,** also called the **Four Stages of Competence,** described by psychologist Abraham Maslow in the 1940's, details how people progress in ability with a new skill. Here's how it works. As you approach something new…take learning to drive a car, for example, you move from complete ignorance to ultimately being able to drive well without even thinking about it. These are the stages:

UNCONSCIOUS INCOMPETENCE – relates to not knowing how to do something, and also not knowing what you're missing. It can be said to be, 'you don't know what you don't know.' Before you began learning about driving a car, you existed in this zone. Where résumé mastery is concerned, this is where you may have been before picking up this book. You had no idea to what degree your résumé was poor and lacked the skill to fix it.

CONSCIOUS INCOMPETENCE – describes your state when you learn what it takes to do something competently, but lack the ability. You now, 'know what you don't know'. In our driving example, as you first take lessons you discover how many things there are to pay attention to behind the wheel, and how inept you are at it. With résumés, as you conclude this chapter and at points throughout this book where you are introduced to new areas of the résumé and their importance, you will begin to operate in this area.

CONSCIOUS COMPETENCE – This stage refers to your understanding of what it takes to be competent, and, with conscious effort, achieving success doing it. With your lessons complete you drive well, but with great concentration and attentiveness. Completing this book and following the steps laid out will bring you directly to this point in résumé creation.

UNCONSCIOUS COMPETENCE – This is the final step wherein you know something well enough that you can do it competently without conscious effort. You are on 'autopilot' and your knowledge and practice bring you success without having to give it your full attention. You can easily drive your car unerringly without a thought about it!

After you internalize the information in this book and begin to see its real-life application, your skill at résumé creation will reach beyond conscious competent. Your choices, focus, and overall job search and professional understanding will increase because you will not only have a great résumé, you will understand what companies look for in a new employee. You will be able to guide yourself into better and better positions in future roles. You will fine-tune your skill over time and eventually you will pick up useful information and incorporate positive changes into your résumé and career, without necessarily being aware of how it happened.

The culmination of mastery with the Five Master Keys will lead you to develop a skill for not only understanding what is needed to create your own successful résumé, but also how those of your peers are lacking, should you choose to help them. You will better scrutinize the résumés of your potential new hires. You will develop a 'gut feeling' about what needs to be included, reflecting your attainment of a level of unconscious competence that will benefit you for your entire career.

Heck, you don't even have to believe that this will happen…it just will.

So let's get to it.

Where to Gain Knowledge

The media is awash in 'helpful' information for the job hunter. Internet searches using tags such as 'job hunting' or 'résumé help' result in **tens of millions** of hits. The hyper-availability of material may contribute to the paralysis many searchers complain about. Where to go? Who to trust?? What am I missing???

Relax. Deep breath in…

Let's go over some of the most popular sources of information for the hopeful applicant and lay them out clearly.

Books

A book, or even **some** books, will likely be your **best** source of information. Why? Well, people don't just write books for the fun of it. Certainly, many people **start** writing a book for the fun of it…but working right through to completion is an arduous task. Millions of books by millions of hopeful authors sit unfinished on hard drives and in desk drawers. It takes a lot of time and effort and, when correctly done, a lot of research to put together a worthwhile nonfiction text. People most often write books because **they have something valuable to say.**

Résumé books, specifically, are written by people who feel they have enough expertise to help job seekers write a great résumé. Whether the book fulfills its objectives notwithstanding, reference books are designed to help, and are very often packed with useful information.

And yet so few people take advantage of this powerful educational medium! Our poll suggested that less than 9% of all applicants who built their own résumé read a knowledgeable text to teach them how. It's no coincidence that much less than 9% of all applicants are considered to have an excellent résumé and get a call to interview!

During my research I read quite a few books on résumé building. Knowing that technology has increasingly impacted virtually every area of résumé development, I chose only to read books that were published within the last six years. That way, I determined, I could ensure that the information remained recent and relevant.

After reading through them I was surprised to discover that the advice in many was already obsolete. Texts just five or six years old taught a job hunter to fax, scan, or snail mail résumés…the sort of thing that would be a waste of time for you to learn about today. Even four-year old books discussed the value of producing a résumé in ASCII or rich text format for scanners to interpret.

Outdated information!

Three years.

If the book you're reading about résumés is older than three years and hasn't been updated, it's not the best, most relevant book for you.

You may glean some important basic information, as some wisdom stands the test of time...but on the whole you will be working with out of date tools.

Articles

Magazine and newspaper articles covering résumé issues can be insightful and provide some important and current tactics. Unfortunately, there is often not enough space or content given in a magazine or newspaper to make it your main source of information. Not only that, newspaper and magazine articles are designed flashy to sell. The **'Top 10 Résumé Mistakes That Will Cost you Your Next Job!'** is a catchy, sexy title for an article, and it may have some great ideas, but it's just a byte-sized look. Reading that article may give you an idea or three, but it's just a nip and tuck when you likely need a full résumé rebuild.

Taken as they are, the average job hunter may garner some advice that helps tighten or improve their résumé in such articles. Do not place all your stock in the advice of one piece, however! If you read five lists of **'Top 10 things...'** you're likely to find vast differences in attitude and opinion between authors.

You may learn worthwhile **tactics** in such articles, but not a sound complete **strategy.** Using effective action words on your résumé is an example of a tactic that can work, a single approach used to create an advantage. Strategy, however, is the overall plan, carefully thought out with the most up-to-date information and executed with the greatest efficiency and effectiveness. It takes more than tactics to win a war; victory requires a brilliant total strategy. This book aims to provide your strategy, complemented by hundreds of tactics proven to work.

Radio

On occasion a radio call-in show will feature an experienced career or employment professional to give their perspective. Hosts are responsible for bringing in guests who speak to relevant issues, and employment challenges are a perennially hot topic. I would highly recommend tuning in when such shows run. Better yet, call in and try to have your own questions aired. Caller concerns will reflect the current employment market and present-day subjects.

These stations don't just let anyone sit as a professional guest, so they will very likely have industry credibility. Remember, however, that they are just one source and may have their own personal opinions that aren't necessarily reflected in recruiters from the kind of company to which you would like to apply.

Job Fairs

Attending job fairs is another great way to gain insight into creating a quality résumé. Often the presentations, workshops, and sessions are valuable, and can provide advice on numerous job-search related issues all under one roof. In fact, there is often an overwhelming amount of information, and zealous job hunters may find themselves buried beneath a growing pile of business cards, brochures, company portfolios, and swag.

Keep in mind that while some associations and governmentally-supported organizations have a mandate to help members find jobs, others are competitive businesses who will clamor for your attention. Some job fair vendors are only there to encourage you to pay for their services.

Recruiters: Agency Wisdom

While there are layers of protection separating you from company or **corporate** recruiters, *agency* recruiters can be outstanding sources of information. They, like their corporate counterparts and more than any other professional, are on the front line of the employment battle. Finding talent, interviewing, sending strong candidates to companies for interviews, and negotiating offers, they survive or perish on their ability to join quality applicants with client companies looking for great new people.

The challenge only becomes clear when we understand that **they don't work for you.** Later this chapter we'll spend more time covering recruiters, and before you close this book you will know how to make them eager partners in your job search.

The Internet...Thar Be Dragons!

If you choose to further your education through the Internet, it comes with a weighty caveat: not all information is created equal! While the Net is teeming with information on résumés, and thousands of 'experts' vying for your attention, you must consider the source. Where does their information come from? What is their background? Look for specific credentials and history before you even consider taking any advice seriously. Many sites simply take articles from other, more reputable sources and don't provide the correct credit. I was recently interviewed by a popular online magazine and gave some advice on job searching techniques. Less than a month later I found my exact words on another site and the alleged expert used not only my quote, but those from numerous other professional sources as their own content!

> *A recent study found that almost 50% of everything on the Internet is made up or false. If you find that hard to believe then you're right because I just made it up. No one checks the validity of most information on the Internet so use your best judgment!*
> Neil Kouba— Senior Associate, Pivotal Integrated HR Solutions

Not cool.

I have found that while many sites on the Internet covering résumés are current and updated regularly, the quality and sources of information in most cases is highly suspect. I visited twenty sites recently to evaluate the sample résumés of supposed specialists. Only **two** came close to reflecting the wants of genuine recruiters based upon our research. Page after page was awkwardly designed, and while some of them I would consider good, most were fair, and a couple were downright poor. Not one was **excellent** based upon the experience and expectations of we Résumé Success 600 members!!

No wonder we recruiters receive so many poor résumés...the Internet is rife with poor advice!! Information for résumé creation and job hunting as a whole is readily available. Too readily, in fact. Always check the source, their credibility, their intentions, **and your own instincts.**

What is a Résumé, REALLY?

The word **résumé** is from the French, meaning **'summary'**. This is different from the **curriculum vitae** or CV, which is Latin for **'course of one's life.'** It's important to mark the differences, because while many people use the two terms interchangeably, they are actually very different in form and audience. A résumé is a distillation of everything you are professionally into a few pages. It is a synopsis. A summary. A CV, on the other hand, can be 10 pages or more in some instances. It is a robust, detailed document, and most often reserved for use in scientific, academic, and medical environments.

Let's have a look at the **real** purposes of a résumé. Don't go checking Webster's or Oxford dictionaries for these definitions, they come from a much higher authority...recruiters who screen your résumé.

> 'To give a brief synopsis of a candidate's skills, education, experience, and accomplishments.'

> "A résumé should be a synopsis of the candidate's career history, education, and career accomplishments."

The above explanations, taken from recruiters from the **Résumé Success 600** surveys read very much like what you might imagine a textbook definition to be. They are absolutely correct. But have a look at those below and see how they differ (I've underlined key parts):

> "It is the single, most important *marketing* document a person will ever create."

> "The purpose of a résumé is to *grab attention and entice* a recruiter to place that first call to a candidate."

> "To start the *sales cycle*."

Hmmm, a very different tale. Rather than an objective description, these answers reflect the subjective candidate's perspective, **your** side of the interpretation; what a résumé is for **you.** This is what recruiters know to be **your purpose** in creating and submitting a résumé. Also, all perfectly true. Finally, have a look at this last group:

Think of your résumé as your first impression. You want to ensure that it truly reflects who you are in hopes of getting an interview.
Peter Ciccia—
Fairmont Hotels
& Resorts

'To highlight how the applicant's previous experience and skill sets fit with *our position*."

"To *enable the hiring manager the ability to assess* if the candidate has the correct technical skill sets to do the job."

"To quickly demonstrate the highlights, achievements, and strengths that *a candidate can bring to our position*."

"Presentation of education, work experience, and *why the candidate should be considered for the position*."

> The purpose of a résumé is to grab attention and entice a recruiter to place that first call to the candidate.
> Sarah Chapman— Director of Western Canada Pivotal Solutions, Canada

This last group has a different focus; they define a résumé based upon the perspective, wants, and needs of the **recruiter**.

Which is correct?

All were asked the same question: **'What is the purpose of a résumé (in your own words)?'** They are **all** correct. You see the inherent challenges in understanding what makes a résumé great? The definition changes depending upon where you sit at the table. You must understand the fundamental purpose of a résumé because it is the real starting point. For this reason the first definitions are true.

More than this, the real purpose of a résumé for **you** it is that it is a sales document; a marketing tool. It is a distillation of everything you are professionally laid out to reach that next step.

> For *you*, the applicant, there is *one* meaning and purpose for a résumé: it is a sales/marketing document used to get an interview.

INSIDER SECRET

The final set of definitions comes at the question from the **recruiter** side. They want the ability to fully assess you, to screen you in or out, to get an idea of whether or not you match their own corporate culture. It sure is a different definition, but it's also 100% right.

Most information on creating a successful résumé stops at the subjective applicant side. They primarily cater to the needs and wants of the applicant. They avoid tackling the most challenging and yet essential opinions, the recruiter's subjective beliefs, because they simply don't know what recruiters want. And recruiters don't go out of their way to teach people what they like to see.

The résumé may be your ball, but it's their ballgame, played in their corporate park. If you break the rules, or even bend them far, make up your own or try to rewrite them, you could be stuck on the bench for a painfully long time. Play by **their** rules, however, and you can win!

Two Ways to Your Best Résumé

There are only two ways to possess an excellent résumé: **build it yourself** or have a **professional build it for you.** If you choose to craft it yourself this book will provide everything you need. There are no shortcuts. It will require work on your behalf, and time, but less than you might think. The result will be the most important document in your professional career and it will be outstanding. As we move through the **5 Master Keys to Résumé Success** you will absorb the knowledge and develop the skills required to follow through effectively.

Your résumé is your personal brand in print. Take it seriously, invest in it, and it will pay off. Ignore it or treat it like everyone else treats theirs and you be seen as just like them…a commodity.

Many people elect to have someone else create their résumé for them. Time constraints, lack of personal interest or confidence compels them to entrust their most vital business document to a professional résumé preparer. This can work extremely well, as there exists a number of quality companies and individuals that honestly do strive to create a world-class résumé and pride themselves on the personal touch. Most others, however, do not, and are clearly out to make a fast buck. With volume services, largely automated processes, impersonal contact, and lack of ongoing support, they prey upon the insecurities of the job seeker.

You can certainly have an excellent résumé created through a few of these services, but it takes some research to separate the wheat from the chaff. Unfortunately, by then the time savings you thought you'd realize by asking another to prepare your résumé or the opportunities you were considering may have evaporated. It is, however, an extremely important first step in your résumé process should you choose this route. Please, if you **do** decide to commit to a résumé service company, allow yourself the time to do your research.

Things to Ask if You Choose to Hire a Professional

If you decide to hire a service to craft your résumé, there are some important questions to have answered in order to properly qualify them. How much do they charge? Prices can vary from $50–$2,000, with executive résumés primarily at the upper end of this range. Be aware that while you don't necessarily need to pay thousands to have a great résumé made for you, the discount services work on volume, and so they will be much less likely to do multiple edits, speak with you personally, address your concerns with sincerity and patience, and have the credentials that you are looking for to feel confidence in them and stand by their work. You are paying for their time and expertise, and their professional brand should be on the line every time they take on a new client. Cheap, cut-rate, volume-based, impersonal companies will charge little…and give little as a result.

Free Résumé Evaluation?

You may have seen this offer online. You send your résumé and they tell you what's wrong with it for free! Sound too good to be true? It often is. You need to realize that for many companies this is simply a sales technique. Sending in your résumé makes you a qualified sales lead, and they'll try to get you to pay for their service. This isn't necessarily a bad thing, and if you have a résumé that needs proofing this can help. They may find spelling errors and so on you have missed. However, aside from the obvious mistakes, their take on what makes your résumé less than great will be their own opinion, and should you send it for a free evaluation to a number of services you'll find that the results are very different. I suggest that you scrutinize your sources, perhaps even speak with a counselor there, **then** decide if you want to send in your résumé for an evaluation. Trust your instincts…many online portals rely upon advertising revenue, volume submissions, and dubious sales techniques. One final thing…they will **always** find something that needs fixing.

Credentials?

A potential résumé service provider should have the appropriate background in recruiting to know what companies want. Someone who is building your résumé should have been a recruiter in at least one company to have an inkling as to what recruiters want in a résumé! They should also possess some education that gives them the credibility to assess and edit English communication, and ideally a combination of both.

There exists a group of designations concerned with résumé creation such as a Certified Professional Résumé Writers (CPRW), Certified Résumé Strategist (CRS), Certified Personnel Consultant (CPC), Credentialed Career Master (CCM), Nationally Certified Résumé Writer (NCRW), among others. Fully half the books I researched were written by people with such designations, and the other half by uncertified authors.

I found neither group better nor worse than the other; some were quite good and some were poor. **Remember that almost NO company or agency recruiters have this qualification and certainly don't require it;** their education is more likely squarely in the Human Resources area, not résumé preparation. However, if you are questioning the background of a résumé service and wondering if they are credible, then their certification by one of the above governing bodies may give you some peace of mind because the organization will often accept accountability for its members' actions in the marketplace. I have found that a number of the examples they provide online are securely in the **good** category. None of them, however, were **great.**

Consultation?

Any quality résumé service will require that you either have a face-to-face or more commonly a phone consultation. It's vital to connect on a personal level. A résumé may be a reflection of your professional experience but it takes interaction to learn the essence of your real history, desires, and qualifications. Many discount services will simply ask you to fill out a questionnaire, and then send you a résumé in a few days. It may even be completed entirely by a computer program. This may work if you want a fair or average résumé, but not a great one.

Free Consultation? Ask for it even if they don't seem to provide it. Yes, they may try to sell you their services, but their investment in the time to speak with you indicates some personal and professional buy-in on their end. Get a sense for their interest and comfort in working on your résumé. Will the person you consult with be the one building your résumé? You don't want to speak with a tenacious salesperson and then discover that you won't be connecting with the person who's actually creating your precious résumé.

In most cases the best combination is an initial consultation, a series of guided questioning in e-format for preliminary information, followed by at least one and ideally several in-depth discussions.

How Long Does it Take?

Expect up to seven days for a start-from-scratch résumé, with three to five days being the norm. Many résumé companies will offer you expedited service if you're in a hurry for an additional fee. In truth it does take time for a professional to craft an outstanding résumé. It's because there will need to be some genuine back and forth, gathering of information and fine-tuning that cannot be rushed. The appropriate questioning, honing, and back and forth that bring a résumé to the top 5% cannot be automated and quality will come from personal service by someone trustworthy.

Templates

We will cover more deeply the template concept in the Format chapter. For the time being it's important to understand that the online, downloaded, or supplied format template is **fatally flawed.** A résumé from successful creation to submission is FAR more than just words on a page organized correctly but generically. Format, in fact, represents only one of the 5 Master Keys to Résumé Success. Even so, the majority of online templates tested were of a quality so low they threaten the marketability of any applicant who chooses to use them. It is a tactic, often a poorly demonstrated one, and doesn't reflect a successful prevailing strategy.

As we proceed through this book we will be creating a kind of super-template called your personal Master Résumé. It will be infused with the full strength of each of the other Master Key insights. The fact that **you** will build the template, understanding each Master Key area and its value to your job search, personalized for you specifically, and encompassing all the other potent ingredients in a great résumé will unerringly bring it beyond the blandly generic and into that top 5%.

How Many Résumés Should I Have?

Brace yourself.

Sit down.

The truth is that you need a different résumé for **each** and **every** position you apply for!

Some résumé professionals will differ on this point.

They're wrong.

The submission of your résumé, as we'll learn later, needs to be a laser beam, not a shotgun blast. A shotgun will hit a wider target and can be submitted to more prospective employers, but with such a diluted force that it will fail to make you distinct from you peers who vie for the same job. With a laser, you know your target well and hit it with your full intent, content, and power…it's a tactic so few job-hunters use that when a recruiter sees it they can't but be impressed. They never fail to impress me as a recruiter.

 INSIDER SECRET — You must target every résumé like a laser for each specific opportunity to attain absolute résumé success.

This is an important Insider Secret so please take it to heart. For each and every role you discover is available, consider, and decide is a strong fit for you, a distinctly new résumé will need to be submitted. Many people submit the same generic résumé to countless roles, thinking that by regurgitating everything they've done in one position they will undoubtedly address any specific needs one particular role might call for…and that's why they don't get called for interview! You must **first** address specifically what they are asking for in their job description. Once you have listed how well you match their priority issues, then you can move on to some more breadth coverage of the job type.

We seem to feel that a résumé should be a reflection of our flexibility as an employee, that we can do anything. This is WRONG. **Great companies DON'T want a jack-of-all-trades** unless they ask for it. Most often they want the person who can do what's on the job posting. Show them you can do that effectively in a great résumé and you will get an interview.

The refreshingly **good news** is that once the Master Résumé is complete, subsequent focused variations for each role will be very easy and take little time.

The Master Résumé

Instead of starting from scratch each time you find a role that appears to be a great fit for you, you will begin with your Master Résumé. The Master Résumé is a complete, powerful document tuned to your abilities, experience, and field. This résumé will be able to stand on its own if you ever need it to; it will be your own professional template. From there and for each specific role we will easily be able to refine it, bringing every subsequent version precisely in line with that company's wants and needs.

While it will take you time as we proceed through this text to create that Master Résumé, the individual résumés for each new role will be straightforward, as you will simply be altering some key information, honestly aligning it more closely with each job description and corporate identity. With minutes of work for each role you will be able to quickly and easily design and redesign your résumé for each company, position, and circumstance.

The Hiring Process

Picture this...

Jane is the Sales Manager at ABZ Inc. She arrives at the office Monday morning, has a chat with colleagues, and settles into her office chair with a mochafrappachino coffee. She turns on her computer, opens her email and, what's this? Someone's interested in the Regional Sales Rep position she had advertised! It's your résumé! She prints it off, returns to her chair, and concentrates her full attention to it. She pulls out a highlighter and pen and makes notes, evaluating your experience. After a good twenty minutes of intense scrutiny, she decides that you are a great fit for the role and calls you. You're thrilled! You interview, and get the job!

This is, of course, an absolute fantasy.

Remember, the hiring manager isn't even the first to see your résumé. The Résumé Gatekeeper most often fills that role. These specialized recruiters are the professionals whose job it is to find new talent for hiring managers who need them. They guard against wastes of time for the manager and themselves; they can open the doors for you or shut you out for good.

INSIDER SECRET — Before your résumé can be considered by the hiring manager, it will likely be judged by the recruiter. Over 90% of résumés never make it past this person.

Here is a more accurate look into their day and your résumé.

Jane is a Sales Manager at ABZ Inc. She's extremely busy with the upcoming merger, sales quotas to be met and a demanding VP. To top it all off, her best Regional Sales Rep just quit. She sends an email to John, who works in Human Resources and does the recruiting for the Sales division.

*John gets the email and sighs. He's already got 11 jobs he needs to fill for demanding hiring managers like Jane. He shoots back a note asking what Jane's timeline is, when she needs this new person. **'Yesterday'** is the one word response. They always say that. John pulls up the company job description for a Regional Sales Rep and uses that to make an ad for an online job board, their own website, and maybe the local newspaper. He's glad there is a job description for this role; sometimes there isn't and he has to make it himself using the hiring manager's often-unreasonable wish list. He minimizes the window and sets a computer alert to remind him to post it by the end of the day. He can't just drop everything for Jane… while some recruiters do nothing but recruit, John is a Human Resources Generalist and has plenty of non-recruiting duties to perform as well. He is always, always busy.*

By 1pm he's moved some things from his desk and the recruiting responsibility is nagging him to get back at it. He opens his inbox again and there are 63 new emails, all résumés for the other jobs he's trying to fill. John starts at the bottom and opens each one, scans it for less than a minute, then imports it to the company Applicant Tracking System (ATS) and deletes it from his inbox. Many of the résumés only get about 5 second glances because they're so poor. Spelling mistakes; delete. Four different fonts: delete. No idea what this person did at their last jobs: delete. Bright orange background and a picture of the applicant: delete.

*By 2:30pm he's through them all, and prints out 6 of them to be contacted. About 50% of the résumés were good enough to **read,** but these six really stood out as excellent and so they're the only ones he'll call in for interview. But that'll be later; he's too busy right now. John grabs a handful of business cards and his suit jacket and heads for a meeting room; he has three back-to-back interviews for an accounting position that also needed to be filled **'yesterday'**.*

At 5:30pm he's back at his desk and finds another 23 résumés in his inbox. No time today, and instead he opens the Regional Sales Rep job description and, using his template, *posts it to a number of websites. While he's doing this Jane calls, wondering if he has any interviews lined up yet; the VP of Sales is putting pressure on. He logs on the Applicant Tracking System again and does a quick search through the tens of thousands of résumés that have been sent to the company in the past. People they already have in the system. He enters the keywords 'sales', 'regional', and sets the parameters to check only his city, around $50,000 income, and only résumés received in the last 6 months. His search pulls 538 résumés. He sighs again and saves the search. It'll have to wait, it's after 6pm and he's got to draft an offer letter to send to a successful applicant tonight.*

The next morning John arrives at the office, turns on his computer and is greeted with 187 résumés in his inbox, and 79 of them are for the Regional Sales Rep job. Your résumé is there, too, number 53 in the long line of résumés to be screened. John reaches for his coffee, rubs his eyes, and starts scrolling through the list.

This story gives you a more realistic look into the world of the corporate recruiter. You must understand it because you want them; **need** them to be on your side. Recruiters are people, just like you. They work very hard under a great deal of pressure from many sides. I recently spoke with a friend of mine who is a recruiter at a large telecommunications company and they had over **four hundred** open jobs to fill.

Busy.

By providing recruiters with a great résumé full of the information they want in ideal form, you make their lives easier, and they'll reward you for it with an interview.

You see, recruiters **want** you to have a great résumé. They would **love** to see great resumes all day, every day because they feel it would make their job easier. Instead of fighting through formatting inconsistencies, poor grammar, and a multitude of other résumé faux pas, they could concentrate on your actual history and what a great new hire you'll be.

But it's not a recruiter's job to help you with your résumé.

> *Remember that the recruiter is the first person to read your résumé and has hundreds of other résumés to read as well. If you make it too cumbersome it may not be read at all.*
> Elise Graziano— Director of Staffing, NetApp, USA

How often have you sent a résumé to a company and had it sent back to you with notes, asking you to fix it up, make a few corrections and then resubmit it?

That's right. Never.

If format, spelling, or any other of the many possible résumé transgressions you will learn about here put off a recruiter, you're likely never to hear from them again. Make their experience reading your résumé a happy one and you'll be surprised at how receptive they will be!

Do They REALLY Read My Résumé?

A fear of the typical job hunter is that when they hit 'send' and their résumé goes out into space, they're never really sure if anyone actually **got** it. When there's no response, the silence can lead one to believe that the recruiter may have missed it. Rest assured, they got it. A key responsibility of a recruiter is to effectively scrutinize **every** résumé and decide who will get an interview.

Recruiters read *every* résumé. So if you send it, they'll read it. Whether they scan and dismiss it immediately or print it, make notes, thoroughly dig into its content, and call you for interview is almost entirely up to *you* and the quality of your résumé.

INSIDER SECRET

RÉSUMÉ SUCCESS 600 SURVEY HIGHLIGHT

A recruiter will decide whether your résumé is worth reading in about 5-seconds. The poor résumés will be screened out here. The résumé next has an average of 57 seconds to prove it's great or it gets filed away and forgotten. With the amount of competition out there for every job, regardless of economic growth or decline, good just isn't good enough.

Have a look at the following chart that shows, according to **Résumé Success 600,** the timeline of your résumé and what can happen to it.

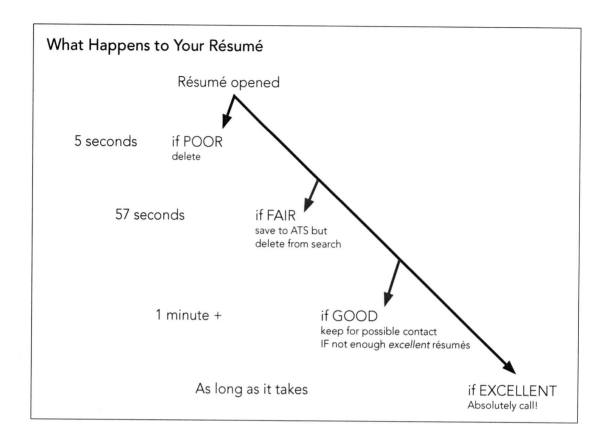

Recruiters are usually extremely good at evaluating résumés they receive. In less than a minute they can tell if you've done your homework, if it's organized well, if it's a generic résumé or tailored to their role, if you're blowing smoke or sincerely talented. Give them a reason to call you and they will. Remember also that your first interview will very likely be not with the hiring manager, but with the **recruiter**. So the Résumé Gatekeeper is important to you beyond even that vital first step with your résumé…It's doubly important to have them on your side!

Recruitment Agencies

A corporate recruiter usually works for the company that needs the new employee, but not always. Sometimes Human Resources responsibilities are outsourced to companies that specialize in staffing, payroll, training, and other HR related roles. In addition, if a company can't find the right talent on their own, or if they're just too busy, they often turn to recruitment agencies who do nothing but recruit for companies in need and are paid based upon their success in getting candidates hired.

Let's get back to John, the recruiter at ABZ Inc. After a period of time screening résumés, interviewing shortlisted applicants, and sending the best few people to meet the hiring manager, he fails to meet a Sales Rep of the quality Jane demands. John might then turn outside the company for help. It's possible his company has a relationship with one, several, or many recruitment agencies.

John would call the agency/agencies, send them the job description, and ask them if they already knew or felt they could find a strong enough candidate to be hired. The agency might have a recruiter or team of recruiters who work specifically on roles for sales professionals. If the mandate is strong the agency will say yes, and then it falls to deciding how much they would be paid if they find the right person. A Fee Agreement would be in place or set up outlining such details, and the agency recruiter(s) would work to **'fill the order'.**

The agency recruiter(s) may have a 'stable' of potential applicants, employed or otherwise already qualified and ready to move to the new company. Or they may post the job on their own website and start a search just as ABZ Inc. did. Most often they do both. Time moves forward, and while the people at ABZ Inc. continue to work at filling the role, the agencies send in their best to John to consider for the position.

These candidates are usually much better than the average ones who submit their résumés to the company itself, because they've already been screened to be a possible fit by the agency recruiter. Good agencies and great recruiters have access to high-quality talent at all times and that's why companies are willing to pay for the hires. The challenge comes when John at ABZ Inc. encounters the myriad of poor recruiting agencies that just recycle mediocre candidates from the same job board sources they themselves have access to, and generally just waste John's time. These are volume-based agencies and, as the name implies, rely on number of submissions and speed to get the placements required to make their agency money. They give the good agencies a poor reputation and are maligned by quality businesses.

A résumé should be clear, concise and appealing to the eye. If I cannot find the information I am looking for in less than 1 minute I will most likely 'file' it.

Melissa Hoover— Recruiter, Honeywell

Excellent résumés are those that speak to you as the candidate for hire within 5 seconds of review, and you can't get to the phone fast enough!

Kim Vu— Recruiting Manager, Compass Group Canada

Most recruitment agencies work on **'contingency'** basis, meaning that if the company doesn't hire someone submitted by the agency, they don't get paid. Agency fees vary according to the fee agreements, which area is being recruited for, and the agency itself. Generally they charge from 15–25% of the new employee's first year salary. If, for example, the agency candidate is screened, interviewed by the recruiter, hiring manager, and other relevant decision makers and approved of, the agency recruiter begins negotiations for the salary, benefits, title, start date and the like for the candidate. If all sides can agree, an offer letter will be drafted by Human Resources and signed by the candidate. If in this case the base salary for the Sales Representative is $50,000 and the agency fee agreement with ABZ Inc. indicates that the fee is set at 20%, it translates to a $10,000 amount for the agency.

Sometimes lower fees or flat rate fees are paid for more junior positions or volume discounts are given for multiple hires or long-standing agreements. Comparatively high fees with relatively little company overhead have resulted in a tremendous surge in the number of recruitment agency businesses, and competition is ferocious.

While most agencies work on contingency, a few work on **retainer.** Executive search agencies generally operate this way, and they ask the company for a fee up front, regardless of their success. If they do find the right hire, they are paid an additional fee when the successful candidate is found. As the name implies, these agencies usually focus on recruiting and placing executive-level candidates.

Recruitment agencies can be a valuable resource for you, but understand that since they only get paid for quality, they only want quality. They often break down their pool of candidates into 'A' candidates (the greats), 'B' candidates (good), and 'C' candidates…(the rest). They will break their backs to market an 'A', work well with 'B's, and disdain hearing from 'C's.

Which will you be? With an outstanding résumé you will be short-tracked to the 'A' category, and if you follow it up with a great interview with them they will move mountains for you!

> *A candidate has less than 10 seconds of my initial attention during screening. Many a great candidate has been missed during this screen because their résumé is poorly representing them. On the flip side, a great résumé will often assist a poorer candidate in grabbing and keeping my attention!*
>
> Janet Chappell—Sr. Recruiter, David Aplin Recruiting, Canada

Agency recruiters will class you as an applicant. The elite group of their candidates, the 'A' candidates, based *first* upon résumé, then upon interview, will *always* be given their greatest attention and they may even 'take you to market', calling their client companies and selling your abilities and talent to them... it's like having your own private marketing team!

INSIDER SECRET

Later on you will learn more about agency recruiters, and how you can use this group to your greatest advantage.

Recruiters Know What They're Doing

Robert McKee wrote an outstanding book on the intricacies of successful movie plots and how they are portrayed called **Story.** In the book he asserted that when an audience member sits down in a theatre to watch a movie, their IQ jumps 50 points as it relates to film. The slightest facial twitch of a character speaks loudly to the alert audience. A glance that lasts a second too long can mean something profound, an almost imperceptible shrug we read easily. It's so true, isn't it?

Well, when a recruiter reads your résumé, it's much like that: if your résumé is poor, it gets that 5 seconds, if it's better, you've got just under a minute. The recruiter will give your résumé that same kind of intense focus as you would give a film. They will read the slightest spelling inconsistency to mean that you aren't detail oriented; the slightest gap in your work history to mean you are hiding something, the lack of promotion over time to mean you lack leadership ability. Whether it's right or wrong, at that point your résumé is all they have and in the hands of a competent recruiter you must assume that they will dissect it quickly and entirely. Our goal then is to give them exactly what they want to see.

They want brilliant.

Times are a Changing

There was a time not too long ago when a vacant job at a company would necessitate the running of an ad in a newspaper. The level of the role and perceived challenges in finding the new hire would often help recruiters decide the size and scope of the placed ad. A junior, common role might earn a small ad in a local paper. Management, and especially executive level roles for the fewer and farther between positions often demanded 1/8, 1/4, or even 1/2 or full page ads in national newspapers who charged upwards of $70,000 for the space!!

The current omnipresence of the Internet and its job banks, boards, and sites allow that same company to advertise themselves for a fraction of the cost and reach a potential candidate anywhere on the planet.

On the surface this may seem like a boon for a company looking to get the word out. It also means, however, that the volume of résumés, which are primarily poorly-suited for the role, choke a recruiters inbox and further add to their busy lives. This is one of the reasons for the popularity of recruitment agencies, who ease the burden in time, effort, and bring highly-specialized recruitment focus to assist.

> *Think of your résumé like an advertisement—when there's so many of them out there, you have to ensure that yours really stands out!*
>
> Maxine Clarke— Sr. Manager of Talent Development, EPCOR

The Need for Résumés

The need for résumés has actually **increased** over time. Even in this highly technological world, a real, physical hard copy résumé is still king. Yes, you may email your résumé to a company to be considered for a job, but if it's great and they want to bring you in for interview, they'll print it out so that they can take it into your meeting, and use it to take notes and answer questions they may have.

But there's another reason for the need of résumés in today's hiring process: discrimination. Nepotism, or granting favor to friends or relatives without merit, sometimes does occur in the employment process. A manager could interview 50 potential candidates and then hire his son and that's fair game. Sad, but while this does occur, applicants are protected by law in important ways.

Human rights law protects certain historically disadvantaged groups of society against discrimination in hiring. If, for example, Bob has accessibility challenges due to a lower back issue which forces him to use a wheelchair, a prospective new employer cannot disqualify him from candidacy due to his impairment. If Bob discovers that a less-qualified candidate was hired he could well file a complaint claiming a human rights violation and things might get very ugly for the company.

The résumé, along with the cover letter, interview, recruiter, and hiring manager notes, all provide a clear, methodical, and largely unbiased paper trail for a company to keep in order to ensure fairness and insure against such liability.

Similarly, in submission to governmental roles there exist rules to protect an applicant. If a federal role requires a specific university or college degree, then **all** applicants possessing that degree must move forward to the next stage of the hiring process. It may not be education; it could be a prior role title, or a designation, or years of experience. The more your résumé resembles the posted job description, the safer you are against possible discrimination for whatever reason.

You see then that the close alignment of a **laser-focused résumé** with a posted job description proves not only attractive to a recruiter for the fit and increases the likelihood of an interview, but protects you from being unfairly kept from moving through the process.

RÉSUMÉ SUCCESS 600 SURVEY HIGHLIGHT

98% of all professional jobs today require a résumé.

That's not all that has changed significantly. Whereas having just a couple of jobs your entire life meant that résumés of the past could easily fit on one page and that was the expectation, the résumés of today are necessarily longer. I only know of one recruiter who still believes that a résumé should be one page, and he's a bit of a throwback. In the late 1980's a two-page résumé became the 'new normal'. In the past few years even this standard has changed, and now many recruiters find that a tight three-page résumé is completely acceptable. In most cases four or five pages is too long, and I advise against it. However, some recruiters will accept even this!

RÉSUMÉ SUCCESS 600 SURVEY HIGHLIGHT

Surveyed recruiters in the Résumé Success 600 felt the following is **too long** for a résumé:

> 1% – 2 pages or more
> 21% – 3 pages or more
> 52% – 4 pages or more
> 23% – 5 pages or more
> 3% – 6 pages or more

Note: No recruiter claimed they would discount a résumé 4 pages or less based on its page count!

The Future of the Résumé

Will we always have résumés? Even as you read this, a shift is taking place, moving away from the traditional résumé application. The first move was to abandon the hand-delivered résumé for the posted option. Then came fax machines, which shared the responsibility of delivery with snail mail, or traditional post. The most significant shift in the past twenty years has been the move to electronic submission via email.

Today, the most recent phase involves the use of **Applicant Tracking Systems**. These programs can identify keywords on your résumé and evaluate your match based on any number of parameters they choose to search from. A disadvantage is that if your résumé doesn't get a high enough **'hit'** rating, you may be kicked out of the process early. Also, the web portals that accept résumés sometimes suffer glitches that really do lose your résumé; a timed-out page may leave you thinking it got through and it's hard to call a computer and ask it if it has your document. We'll get around these issues later. The upsides to the Applicant Tracking System, or ATS, is that while you may not be a match for the role you applied for, the software may identify you as a strong fit for another role at the company you didn't even know was available! Also, these companies will keep your résumé for months, some as long as a year before purging, leaving future opportunities open.

What's next? A growing number of organizations are developing complex web portals that ask you specific questions about your education, history, and career experience. Instead of posting a job description, getting an e-résumé and then having the recruiter or tracking software search the résumé for a possible match, they will screen people out at the source. Picture a combination of a résumé and an application form filled out online. Complex algorithms will evaluate your match to the job based on preset criteria. Recruiters might not even see your application/résumé if it doesn't get a high enough rating by the program.

Don't be discouraged though! The résumé is and will remain vital in your search for the foreseeable future.

At this point in history the résumé is more important now than ever. It has evolved into the ultimate tool in both your personal job search and a company's screening process. Environmental preservation might lead to the loss of a paper résumé; technological advancement may dissect its content; law and process may alter its constituent parts, but since the résumé is a snapshot of your professional life in its most powerful form, its need will remain.

The résumé is here to stay.

Keywords

As screening techniques become more automated, the idea of keywords and their use in making the résumé a strong fit for a posted job has become en vogue. The idea is simple: the computer will search your résumé for specific words to give it a 'hit rating' or ranking. Not only can independent computer programs and systems do this, but also on the Internet, job sites send out 'robots' or 'bots' to 'spider' web servers for keyword matches. These programs, designed to perform monotonous, time-consuming searches at many times human speeds, efficiently scan web information that aid their master in finding keyword hits. People have tried to take advantage of this automated search technique.

Know that keywords are important these days as Applicant Tracking Systems save recruiters time by searching for specific skills by word. Instead of just laundry listing the key words, embed them in your bullet points as descriptors for the work you did.
Elise Graziano— Director of Staffing, NetApp, USA

The shortcut: add a section on the résumé with all words you think a computer would key in on and add them there, targeted and numerous, the idea of the keywords section was to trick the computer screening your résumé to think you were the perfect fit with a high 'match' rating. The problem? As much as a computer can be a useful tool in finding how your résumé matches what a company is looking for, in the end the recruiter still scans it. And they **hate** it when you try to trick them. Wouldn't you?

The need to understand keywords remains, though, and you **will** use them, just honestly. In fact, in the Content section we will go over how to use this powerful screening process to your advantage in matching, while remaining on the recruiter's good side.

Okay, let's get to work!

STEP 1a: Register a new email address exclusively for use with your job search

1 out of every 10 résumés I get from junior candidates or students comes with a highly unprofessional email address. What are people thinking?

Maya Toussaint— Recruiter, Yellow Pages Group

You are going to get a lot of mileage out of your email address during your job search, adding it to your résumé, e-submitting documents, registering on job sites, and so on. In order to avoid having valuable, even vital employment-related messages being lost amongst your other mail, you should register an email address **specifically** for use in your job hunt.

More importantly, your email address is a small but significant reflection of your overall application to a recruiter. It can be a real sore spot for them if you're not careful. If you have a current email that can possibly be interpreted as inappropriate, you **cannot** list it on your résumé. If your friends send you notes at **sexykitty29@hotmail.com** or similarly risqué tags, a recruiter may find it hard to take you seriously. It's easy to set up a new and free email address at countless sites. Your current regular provider likely offers numerous free additional addresses with your account, so you could use one of those.

If you try to enter your personal name as your address, it will likely have been taken already. Alas, you're probably not the only person with your name! Instead, add something relevant and professional. **davidjgardner@gmail.com** will likely be taken. If I were in the sales profession, I could choose **davidjgardner_sales@gmail.com,** which is more likely to be available and provides an easily remembered and convenient address to which your job search contacts can be stored. You can separate parts of the address with an underscore mark, or "_".

Avoid using an email address with a lot of numbers. **Johnsmith 684734@gmail.com** may be available and offered by the email company as an option, but since *most spam email comes in this form,* the filters of most companies will not let it through.

Going forward use only this address for all résumé and correspondence so you can keep pertinent information in one, useful place.

What is 'FIT'?

In the field of recruiting we often throw around the word **'fit'**. A fair definition for fit might be **'an individual's appropriateness for a position'**. The reasonable question then arises, 'Appropriateness according to **whom and what are the criteria for deciding??'** Of course your own belief of what might be a fit for **you** is important, and we'll deal with that shortly, but again we need to shift the focus and fully appreciate the **company's** perspective. You will need to grasp **their** needs in order to be most effective in identifying the best opportunities for yourself.

Your résumé will be the first contact with them, and they will attempt to determine your fit based upon its content alone. Do you have the right number of years' experience? Do you have the right educational background? At this point they are only looking to screen and evaluate based upon the 'paper' you. An evaluation that is vital because it will either lead to the next step or the loss of the opportunity.

Later, when you interview face-to-face, they will be looking for the other aspects of fit including personality, character, ambition, corporate culture, presence, teamwork, loyalty, and a host of other criteria a savvy recruiter will use to evaluate you. You will be able to give them a tantalizing glimpse at this side of you in your résumé submission through your cover letter, which you will learn about in Chapter 7.

What Does Your Next Position Look Like?

Even if you believe to have found a number of positions you would like to apply to before picking up this book, let's back up and understand, based upon fit, what that next job might realistically look like.

If you go to job boards or even search the newspaper classified ads to look for jobs you **think** you **could** do, you're already off to a poor start. While you will find many, you may be **well qualified** for only a few. Recruiters don't want candidates who are 100% interested but only a 20% fit for the role they're working on. They want 66% or more, but over 80% is ideal. Remember, a laser, not a shotgun. You must be realistic based upon what you've done already. If you left the workforce and started your own small company and gave yourself the title of CEO, it doesn't mean that you are instantly qualified to be a CEO in the next company you apply to. Think of what your next job **should** be. What makes sense and flows from your current or prior role? If you've been a Sales Manager for one year, you likely won't be seen as a great fit for a Director of Sales role at another company…you just don't have the experience, even if you were wildly successful for that year. It may be better to get another Sales Manager role, but one that's a step up in some way.

Perhaps you aim to join a better/bigger/more well-known company, or one with a better bonus structure, or one that is grooming the Sales Manager to take over the Director of Sales position in a few years. Don't always assume your next move should be one step up the corporate ladder. Even a side step to a similar role can allow you to prove your worth to a new organization. A possible exception here is that if you have been at a large company, to move to a smaller company may give you an earlier shot at a step up.

A two year Sales Manager at a pharmaceutical heavyweight like Pfizer may be able to move to a Director of Sales at a small company. While you are moving up in title here, that won't necessarily mean a raise in income even with the loftier title, as smaller companies are less likely to have the budget to pay top dollar for you. You always want progression, but it might not **look** like a step up on paper. Often a step up to the same title but a larger company will provide you with a better personal brand in the future. Other times a move to a smaller company with a promotion will be a step forward. Realize though, that it is much more difficult to get both a promotion **and** a step up to the next class of company size/branding.

STEP 1b: Consider what your next career position might be

Make a short list of the positions you feel you are qualified for based upon where you've been and what you aspire to be in your next move.

For example, a Sales Manager from a car rental company may be suitable for: *a Sales Representative, Internal Sales, External Sales, Sales Manager, Area Manager, District Sales Manager, Territory Sales Manager,* and others. Remember, while some role titles are the same no matter where you go, many are different depending on the organization. For this reason expand above and below your current qualification area as you consider. A Sales Manager at one company may have several staff to oversee, and a large area to supervise and sell in. At a competing company, this same set of responsibilities may be called a City Sales Manager. You don't want to miss out on a potential opportunity solely because of title incongruence.

Keep this list handy.

STEP 1c: Use the Internet to broaden your list

You may not even know what other jobs require your skill set…they may be simply titled differently. Do a search for not only the titles you know to be associated with your field and level, but also your main career branch and your core responsibilities as you know them. For example, you are in Sales, but only know **Sales Representative, Sales Agent,** and **Inside Sales** to be similar titles. Do an Internet search using *'sales jobs'* or *'sales job titles'* and you will find a host of similar roles that go by different titles. You can also try an Internet search using *'(your title) career path'*. This will likely unearth some other titles that match your career trajectory that you may not have known about.

Add these titles to the ones you have already listed and keep this list.

Consider What Your Great Fit Is

When you are considering what your next role might look like, it's always valuable to know what's most important to you. Many people think that when a person is considering their next move that money rules. **Not true.** When I discuss with my applicants what their priorities are, and really dig deep to find out where their heart is, the number one target is **never** money. The only exceptions are some entry-level jobs wherein an applicant needs to make sure they have money enough to take care of their personal basic necessities.

What ranks number 1? It varies…needs are entirely subjective depending upon what is most important to **you** and only you at that point in your professional life! I have spoken with candidates who would take virtually **any** salary if only they could work within a 15-minute commute from their home. Others have told me that they would take a 25% cut in pay so long as there was long-term potential for growth at a new company. Still other applicants have confided that they would drive up to two hours to the office if only they could step one wrung up the corporate ladder in their move. Again, entirely subjective…so what's important to you?

STEP 1d: Rate your perceived fit

Take a look at the following list of fit criteria and rate them from 1–3, 1 being a priority, 2 representing a good-to-have, and 3 reflecting something that isn't so vital to you.

Higher salary _____

Better location _____

Work/Life balance _____

Top ranked company (Fortune 500 or Top Company to work for) _____

Great leadership team _____

Bigger better company name (brand recognition) _____

Opportunities for growth/promotion over time _____

Working with a strong mentor _____

Immediate promotion ____

Strong/recognized training program ____

Corporate culture ____

Enjoyable work ____

Other _____

If you wrote down 1 for all, go back and be brutally honest with yourself. If you could only write a '1' for three of the above, which would they be?

Have a look at your answers; they're very telling! Now you know what your priorities are, and that knowledge will help you decide what your next best move is.

Now, of the three number '1' answers, choose the top one, the one that you would put all others aside for if you could have it. **That** is your answer! Right now, preparing for the next stage of your professional career, you have your **most important** priority. Keep this close! You cannot afford to move to a new company in a role that isn't in line with this or another top priority because you will end up dissatisfied and unhappy. You will be more likely to want to change jobs again or be let go due to lack of passion or performance. However, if you know that you have chosen your priority and land the job that is in line with it, you stand a much better chance of having success and enjoying your career there!

The first target of your job search must be in line with this priority, but your second and third choices are still very important to you and so if that number one eludes you at first, you can move towards the next top option. You will be pleasantly surprised that with the understanding of what it is you really want, the opportunities that are most closely associated with it will present themselves.

With a new and growing understanding of what will typify a quality professional fit for you, let's test your knowledge of the relevant players in your priority group versus any list you may have already put together for your search.

Keep this prioritized list for current and future reference!

STEP 1e: Brainstorm industries and companies to move toward

Brainstorm a list of the companies and/or industries that you feel may be a fit for you based upon your closest needs as discovered in **STEP 1d** above. If, for example, your top fit area is Bigger better company name (brand recognition), then list all the companies bigger/more recognizable than your last that you know to have a branch, office, or headquarters in your city or town. Don't discriminate on distance, size, or anything at this point, just write as many as you can.

You will likely discover that your list is not very extensive…perhaps you just don't know a lot about what companies in your city meet your criteria most closely…this is expected! Remember Maslow's stages? You're just moving from the unconscious incompetent area to the conscious incompetence. At this point it's important to know that there are things you don't yet know. We'll dig more deeply into this in Chapter 8, but from here on, as you continue with the research needed to complete this book and your exercises, start paying attention to positions and companies that seem in line with your priorities. Add them to your list.

We will expand and use this list in the Submission chapter.

Let's start on some real research that will help you get on the right path to evaluating the best opportunities for you. Don't skip these steps!

STEP 1f: Put together a group of strong, relevant job descriptions

i: Take some time right now to search the Internet for actual job postings in line with your background and priorities.

ii: Visit job boards, register using your new email address, and browse the listing for your job titles.

iii: Visit company websites and find job postings in your area.

iv: Go to recruitment agency sites and do the same. You are searching for those that include the two important job description sections: Experience Required and Responsibilities.

v: Flesh out this group with an Internet search of your standard job title. If you're a Plant Manager, type **'Plant Manager job description'**. You will come up with millions of hits. Take the first few at the top, usually the most popular. These are useful because they will generally encompass the industry norms for what your job should entail.

STEP 1g: Collect the best job descriptions for you

Take 8–12 (yes, that many to be truly diligent) and from them find the best representative descriptions for your next role. You'll find some are better than others. Even if they are out of your commuting range, don't exclude any quality ones. It's important to have a full complement of detailed job descriptions to make this exercise work. Be careful to keep the ones most closely resembling your next move, and not roles you feel you would **like** to move toward. Adaptation of your résumé for individual opportunities will come later.

STEP 1h: Print these job descriptions out; we will use them in the next chapter

These searches will be not only great practice for you to be able to find the most appropriate roles to submit to, but it will also expand your knowledge of the types of responsibilities and experience that companies are demanding for the role you consider.

This chapter has provided you a general foundation of knowledge to ensure your résumé will be top-notch, but this is just the beginning! In many ways its purpose is to tantalize you, to stimulate you to start asking the relevant questions in your job search that will put you ahead of the pack. Throughout the following chapters you will continue to build your knowledge base. Consider the rest of this book an extension of this section, expanding your understanding of the processes and product that makes a successful résumé.

Next stop: Experience!

Chapter 2 Summary

Master Key #1: KNOWLEDGE

- Maslow's Stages of Learning

- Information can be found in books, magazine and newspaper articles, Internet, recruiters, and job fairs. Be wary of the source

- A résumé is:
  - In general: A summary of experience, education, and skills
  - For applicant: A sales/marketing document to get an interview
  - For Recruiter: The tool used to screen in/out applicants for interview

- To have a top 5% résumé have one built by a recognized expert **or** Build one yourself using recognized expert advice

- Standard templates are generally very poor and only represent a part of what makes a successful résumé and submission

- Evaluate a résumé expert to build your résumé with: qualifications, consultation, follow-up, and price

- Craft a Master Résumé, then use it as a guide to tailor-make every submitted résumé

- The first and most important point of contact between you and a company is the Résumé Gatekeeper, whose job it is to weed out 90% of lesser quality résumés and shortlist about 5–9% for interview

- So long as they are submitted correctly a recruiter reads **every** résumé

- Recruitment agencies are hired through contingency or retainer to find suitable candidates for a company job search if that company needs help; they are usually paid for successful candidates only

- Recruiters are very good at knowing what they want in a résumé, and it's not their job to help you improve yours

- Résumés help by creating a hiring process paper trail important to avoid discrimination and encourage equality

- Résumés are moving to full electronic format through application portals, and the essential ingredients of a top résumé still apply directly to this new medium

- Determine the best fit company/industry/area for your priority interests and existing talents

- Start learning about job descriptions that concern your professional area/companies and what they ask for/areas that may work for you

Chapter STEPS

STEP 1a: Register a new email address exclusively for use with your job search

STEP 1b: Consider what your next career position might be

STEP 1c: Use the Internet to broaden your list

STEP 1d: Rate your perceived fit

STEP 1e: Brainstorm industries and companies to move toward

STEP 1f: Put together a group of strong, relevant job descriptions

STEP 1g: Collect the best job descriptions for you

STEP 1h: Print these job descriptions out; we will use them in the next chapter

It's critical to have a strong, deep, and full understanding of your professional experience in order to be able to align yourself perfectly to the requirements of a new job.

Tom Rainey
—Executive Recruiter,
Novus Reputo Recruiting

chapter 3

Master Key #2: EXPERIENCE

Many people argue that your prior experience is the only important thing you have to convey to a recruiter in order to qualify for an interview and job. Say, for example, you worked at a company that operates in an industry similar to the one you are applying for, or perhaps even a direct competitor, and engaged in a similar role. It seems reasonable that they would be thrilled to meet you. You already fit, right?

Not by a long shot.

Experience listed on a résumé is an excellent indicator of your potential fit for a new role, but the places you worked comprise only a part of the important experiential information a skilled recruiter considers. Education, responsibilities, successes, challenges, reports, recognition, projects, scope, professional development, awards, and peripheral skills represent just a short list of the many constituent parts of a robust, powerful experience set.

Your experience is unique. No one will have the same specific background as you, so this represents a profound way you will differentiate yourself from your competition in the marketplace. To be true, even someone with an identical background professionally can have a startlingly different set of experiences on their résumé, and should!

Experience Presentation is Vital

On the surface it seems as though this is an area where little outside help can be supplied. A book such as this one may help you master the creation of an excellent résumé, but it surely can't give you great experience if you possess none, right?

Not necessarily!

Remember, a résumé is a **marketing** document from your side of the table. Where you worked, when, and what you did are essential. However, the **packaging** of that information is something that can make all the difference. I've seen résumés that outline an outstanding pedigree of high profile companies as past employers; but I couldn't tell what they **did** there! The poorly outlined responsibilities, lack of quality areas of impact, failure to take credit for success, and general blandness convinced me time and again that working for those strong companies wasn't enough to bring such candidates in to interview.

So I wouldn't.

I've also seen résumés wherein the applicant had worked for not a single employer I recognized, and yet their experience was laid out so vividly and powerfully that I felt compelled to call them in.

So I did.

No, we can't change your experience, but what we **can** do is take good, average, or even poor overall experience and present it in such a way that is **so** clear, articulate, relevant, and powerful, that employers will still send you to the short list of candidates to get that interview call.

How you present your experience raises or lowers the perceived level of *fit* a recruiter feels you have for that job/company…it's *not* just about *what* your experience is.

What Did My Company DO, Anyway?

When a recruiter first opens your résumé, they scan the names of the companies at which you've worked. Perhaps they recognize the names, perhaps they don't. What they're looking for is how germane they are relative to the job they're recruiting for. Ideally, they would love to scrutinize each company for industry, sector, size, scope, market position, revenue and other company traits to best define the fit, but they have neither the time nor often the expertise to do such an analysis.

If your last employer was a household brand name company that will help them consider relevance, but it still doesn't mean that the résumé gatekeeper has a clue the kind of clout they have in the industry and if it suits you well for their role. For this reason you must have a **complete grasp** of your experience and do more than just list the company. If you come from a 'real estate' company, it makes a difference to a hiring manager if you were responsible for Accounts Payable at a $50,000 private real estate office or at a $3.4B real estate development firm!

The better the company you come from, the better **you** are. That organization hired you and cultivated your talent. It's vital to know the details about your past companies for both your résumé and interview.

So, how well DO you know your past employers?

Company Synopsis:

STEP 2a: List important details of prior employers

Using the following template, or on a separate piece of paper, provide details of your employers beginning with the most recent. We will use this information later to create an outstanding miniature company profile to help recruiters evaluate you properly…and positively!

Company name: _____

\# of employees: _____

\# of facilities: _____

Local/national/international: what cities, states, provinces, countries: _____

Place in industry vs competitors: _____

Private/public/traded where: _____

Years in business: _____

Interesting facts/firsts: _____

Annual Revenues: _____

Annual Sales: _____

Awards/Recognition: _____

Other: _____

As you work through this list, it may strike you that the answers don't come quickly. In fact, you may not be able to answer but a fraction of them.

How can you convince a recruiter, through résumé or interview, that your experience is a fit if you don't know where you've been??

Executive level job hunters will likely have had access to much of this information, but that does not exempt them from additional study! They must be required to know even higher-level intimate knowledge of the company and industry. Financials, past history, future plans, mergers/acquisitions, trends, global interests…executives, too, must be highly knowledgeable about companies they participated in leading.

You need to know! Why?

First of all the contents of this list will help you create the **Company Synopsis** area of your résumé. This highly-informative summary of what your past companies represent in their market is a part of the larger Experience section of your résumé, and is invaluable to recruiters.

RÉSUMÉ SUCCESS 600 SURVEY HIGHLIGHT

Company Synopsis is a section of Experience that less than 5% of job hunters include on their résumé…and yet over 92% of recruiters surveyed LOVE to see it!

In addition, having a solid factual grasp of your prior employers provides you great ammunition for your interview at a new company. You can favorably compare any aspect of your potential new employer with your old, and use this information to discuss similarities that show your competence, or dissimilarities that show you're eager to move into different and challenging waters. Recruiters love candidates at every level who are savvy enough to learn both minute and big picture implications their role has on the organization and market.

If you struggle to come up with the answers to these above questions, head to the company website, and search elsewhere on the Internet. For all but the smallest of organizations, company information will be easy to come by. For additional help, contact a close associate or colleague at that company. If you left on good terms, your employer should be able to help you, once you explain the reasons why. Some companies will not be able to release all information due to policy, privacy, or protocol issues, but that's fine. Fill in as much as possible.

What DID You Do??

Now that we have grown a deeper understanding of your past companies, let's turn to the responsibilities you were entrusted with.

STEP 2b: Determine what relevant responsibilities you have had

Take out the pile of job descriptions you printed last chapter in **STEP 1h.** Go through them completely and **highlight** every responsibility that you have had in the past at any job. Even if you have only **some** familiarity with that area, highlight it anyway! Also highlight those responsibilities from those roles above and below your current role and others that are entitled differently with the similar responsibilities.

Cut and paste or copy these to another list we'll call the **'Responsibilities Done!'** list

This exercise has a threefold purpose. Firstly, you can readily compare the highlighted responsibilities you have done with the overall duties of that role to see how close a fit you are. Should you pull a job description and find that you've only highlighted 25% of the responsibilities and requirements, then it's likely not a great fit for you at this point in your career.

Secondly, you will use these highlighted roles to help stimulate your memory as you work to fully populate the Responsibilities section for each company in your professional history.

Finally, you will begin to recognize a **pattern** in the experiences they expect you bring to the table, whether you've done them or not. If, for example, 16 of the 20 job descriptions list **'ability to train and lead a team of staff'**, then you know that this is a **key** experiential requirement for your role and you must be certain this is included prominently in your Master Résumé and cover letter.

STEP 2c: Determine what relevant responsibilities you have not yet had

Go through the job descriptions and locate responsibilities that commonly appear for your job title. Cut, paste, or copy these to a list we'll call the **'Responsibilities Needed!'** list. Even if they are not highlighted, meaning you've not yet done them, add all those with multiple hits.

Improving Your Professional Pedigree

This last list is a valuable professional tool for your own use. It provides you with insight into what a company expects for your position, and gives you an idea in what areas you are deficient. The duties that are not highlighted are responsibilities that you must try to make a part of your overall professional package as soon as possible. If taking a course or volunteering can provide it, do it! Some duties you have not yet performed you will need to seek out at your next company. Take on additional responsibilities, ask for mentorship, and you will find a way to add that ability to your growing talent list and create an even stronger match for companies as you progress in your career.

Now let's begin listing the responsibilities you performed with each specific company at which you worked.

Responsibilities Fully Listed

STEP 2d: Fully list responsibilities for prior roles

Use the space below or on in your notebook to list your roles and fully relate your responsibilities for each. If you have the original job description for the role you occupied, that will help as a starting point, but your list will be much longer. Use the duties you just highlighted from the pile of job descriptions to flesh out your list.

As a brainstorm, remember, do not judge or discriminate between major or minor responsibilities you had, just write as much as possible. Don't correct your spelling, try to make correct sentences or organize; just fill out everything you were responsible for! If you are quite new to the workforce, then list volunteer activities and part time jobs. Begin with your most recent/present position.

A résumé is your personal marketing document. It should be targeted. To do this, you need to understand what the requirements are for your next specific career step. With this you can create a truly effective résumé that delivers great results!
Laurie Sterling— Director, Summit Search Group

JOB #1 _____

Responsibilities _____

_____

_____

_____

_____

_____

_____

_____

_____

_____

_____

_____

_____

_____

_____

_____

JOB #2 _____

Responsibilities _____

_____

_____

_____

_____

_____

_____

_____

_____

_____

_____

_____

_____

_____

_____

JOB #3 _____

Responsibilities _____

_____

_____

_____

_____

_____

_____

_____

_____

_____

_____

_____

_____

_____

As the lists grow longer and your flow of ideas begins to ebb, read the following to further stimulate your brainstorming.

- Run through your typical day, what were you responsible for daily?

- Were there weekly responsibilities?

- Monthly? Quarterly? Annually?

- What one time only projects were you involved in?

- Was something new implemented that you participated in?

- Was there an effort to improve something or change something that you were a part of?

- Were you on a team or part of a group or division who were responsible for something?

- Do you have any performance reviews for prior roles? They will often show areas of responsibilities in addition to how well you performed them.

All levels of job hunter will benefit from this exercise. You may find that there are many areas of responsibility that you edited out in earlier résumé versions that are vital to your next and future roles!

Take your time to do this thoroughly. When you're done it should be a long and largely disorganized list. Don't worry! Within this list are the responsibilities you will use on your Master Résumé, and we'll pare them down to their best form later.

Accomplishments Set You Apart

The Accomplishments subsection of a résumé is a powerhouse when it comes to separating you from peers with similar experience. Whereas the Responsibilities list are important to help you reach the minimum qualifications of a role, the Accomplishments list will represent what separates you from everyone else; how you excel. Achievements, awards, recognition, targets met and exceeded, timelines beaten, these are all aspects of the Accomplishments section. Anything you did above and beyond the call, every way you were better than their expectations or your peers, belongs on this list. Were you the #1 Sales Rep four of six months running? Even if you were the #5 rep, but in a group of 45, that's still exceptional…list it!

INSIDER SECRET

The Accomplishments section is one of the most powerfully compelling areas of a résumé for a recruiter. If I were to have five similarly qualified applicants and one includes a strong Accomplishments section, he/she is my first call, *always*…and 8 out of 10 résumés *don't* have it.

You may feel that you had an ordinary job that didn't leave much room for the extraordinary, but if you think deeply enough you can always come up with at least a couple.

STEP 2e: Fully list all accomplishments for each role

Use these as a start and run with it, listing your accomplishments. Don't leave anything off, no matter how insignificant it may seem!

This will help stimulate your memory and creativity:

- How did you save the company money?

- Were you recognized at a meeting or even an Annual General Meeting for something you did?

- Did you make the company money?

- Were you given an award, or a special title for your contributions?

- Was there a process in place that you made better?

- Did you initiate a new process that wasn't there before?

- How were you better than others doing the same job?

- Were you a part of a group or division that was successful?

- Were you promoted?

- Were your performance reviews excellent, or if in some areas, which?

- Did you volunteer to lead a committee or participate in one?

- Did you head up a fundraiser, or did you raise more funds than others?

- Did you receive any awards?

JOB #1 _____

Accomplishments _____

_____

_____

_____

_____

_____

_____

_____

_____

_____

_____

_____

_____

_____

Have you forgotten anything? Go back to the two lists and have another go, put yourself mentally back into the role and recall what the responsibilities were and what you achieved there.

Next, follow this by doing the same brainstorming exercise for your next two most recent positions:

JOB #2 _____

Accomplishments _____

_____

_____

_____

_____

_____

_____

_____

_____

_____

_____

_____

_____

_____

JOB #3 _____

Accomplishments _____

_____

_____

_____

_____

_____

_____

_____

_____

_____

_____

_____

_____

_____

In order to list your other positions, responsibilities, and achievements, should your experience extend beyond three roles, either photocopy this last page, or pull out a lined notepad and record them there. You can, of course record all the brainstorming outside this book on your own paper.

If this is a library book and you wrote right on these pages, you're in big trouble. I'm telling!

Core Competencies: Your Entire Career in a Few Lines

Now we can go back and list the vital points required for what will be your first experiential section on the résumé: your Core Competencies.

STEP 2f: Decide which core areas are most important for you and list

Decide which 6–8 areas are most important to your industry, field, and roles, and list them using the job description list from Step 2b. An example of 5 for a Sales Manager might be:

Leadership, Performance, Growth, Retention, and Improvement

To brainstorm key information for each category, consider the sum of your experience in each core area and list:

Leadership:

- 3 years as Sr. Sales Rep leading team of 4,
- 5 years as Sales Manager
- Attended 3 leadership camps
- Very strong on the team building side
- As sales rep raised bar on sales in my area, showed others, mentored them and they improved
- Big picture thinker throughout career
- Awarded regional leadership prize 1 year.

Don't judge, just list. Do so for each of these areas and save the list.

Again, don't worry about the apparent disarray of these lists, what's important is that you've exhausted your mental inventory of experiences and accomplishments and filled these areas. We'll make them beautiful and drop them into your Master Résumé template very soon.

In the next chapter you will start to see the actual résumé taking shape.

Chapter 3 Summary

Master Key #2: EXPERIENCE

- Packaging and presentation of Experience makes a significant difference in the value of your résumé to a recruiter

- Company Synopsis helps a recruiter compare your history with that of their company in order to find a fit.

- Most applicants neglect to add the Company Synopsis subsection

- Responsibilities should contain, but are not limited to, popular duties known to be required for your new role

- Identifying which duties you have not yet done can help you develop your professional portfolio moving forward

- If you have little match in your responsibilities the job may not be a fit for your current qualifications

- The Accomplishments area is extremely attractive to recruiters and is absent or poorly done on most résumés

Chapter STEPS

STEP 2a: List important details of prior employers

STEP 2b: Determine what relevant responsibilities you have had

STEP 2c: Determine what relevant responsibilities you have not yet had

STEP 2d: Fully list responsibilities for prior roles

STEP 2e: Fully list all accomplishments for each role

STEP 2f: Decide which core areas are most important for you and list

Effective formatting can make an incredible difference to the expression of your work and educational history to a recruiter. Use the right type, full of both simplicity and potency, and doors will open to you!

David J. Gardner

chapter 4

Master Key #3: FORMAT

People sometimes ask me how a recruiter can possibly determine whether or not they are a strong candidate for a job with just that **5-second** initial screening of the résumé. What the recruiter is considering in those moments is, 'Will it be worth my while to read this more deeply?' The criteria they use to decide this involves both content and visual appeal. A powerful format, skillfully used can compel them to stick around to learn more about you every time.

What sections are included and where, fonts, size, page length, white space, subsections, layout of information, organization of content, all affect the recruiter as they scan, then dig into your résumé. Great experience obscured by poor format is usually passed over. As recruiters we want a résumé that's easy to read but contains every piece of information we need to effectively assess you. But equally as important, we want it placed and ordered in a way that makes our task as easy as possible.

Format matters. Let's go over what works, what doesn't, and start to build the framework of your ultimate résumé.

Templates

Tragically, the majority of job searchers, rather then learning how to build a truly great résumé often resort to shortcutting by downloading an online template and simply plugging in the required fields.

You must ask yourself: Who created the template? What was their background? Are their motives sincere or suspect?

Unfortunately, many of the templates evaluated online were poor, generally lacking some of the most important sections that recruiters rely upon. Others were better, but didn't go far enough to bring an applicant's presentation from good to great. Templates found in résumé books were inconsistent, occasionally preaching one way in the text but offering a different strategy in their résumé examples.

Jim Collins begins his outstanding business book, *Good to Great*, with this insightful phrase: **'Good is the enemy of great'.** He meant that it's so hard to become great when good seems fine. Not pushing, learning, growing, innovating, and striving for excellence curses companies to be simply **good,** and never reach their true potential.

It's like that with résumés...and, frankly, you just can't afford to be good when only great gets the call.

The most significant drawback of using a traditional template, as mentioned earlier, is that it attempts to address just one of the Master Keys with the assumption that it is all that is needed. It doesn't increase your knowledge of the process, aid you in streamlining best your experience, provide you with powerful content, or assist you with the best submission strategies. It deals with only format, and that's just not enough to make your résumé better than that of your peers.

Templates by themselves are generic, and you need personal and specific. The mediocrity that standard templates offer can prove fatal to an earnest job search. Recruiters rarely need to take the time to read average.

Format Types

During my research for this book I came across no less than **seventeen** different résumé formats. **Linear, Reordered chronological, Newsletter,**

Creative/Innovative, List, these are all formats that organize information differently, emphasizing some facets of experience and diminishing others. In my years as a recruiter I came across many of these, along with other, stranger combinations. Each was supposedly tailor-made for individual situations the candidate found him/herself in.

Since your background may present opportunities and challenges unique to you, so the logic goes, you should orient and layout your résumé in a way that draws attention to the areas you want to showcase and away from that which you need to conceal.

Do you see what the error is in this way thinking? **You** want to conceal? **You** want to showcase? It's not at all about what you want to show, remember, it's about what the recruiter wants and needs to see. Do you think a busy recruiter considers it a valuable use of time to sift through seventeen different formats to get the information they need from applicants? No. The fewer formats the better for them…meaning the fewer the better for **you.**

> **In fact there's only one true résumé format that gives them information in a structure comfortable for them to read. *The Reverse Chronological Résumé.***

The **Reverse Chronological** format can be used in virtually every situation. Recruiters love to read this style of résumé! In the RC format, the applicant lists roles, starting with the most recent, along with dates, company, and full description of responsibilities while working there. It lets a recruiter easily match the job description with your past responsibilities…in other words it's the best tool for them, so you must use it!

Oftentimes people suggest what's called the **Functional** résumé as a great alternative to the RC format. In this style the applicant emphasizes skills and functions rather than a chronological description of detailed, job-specific experience. At the end of the Functional résumé sits a short list of positions held with dates, but no listing of what the roles actually entailed. This format is a way for a candidate to display the general skills they bring to the table. The idea is that if a company needs leadership, for example, they will find a list of leadership experiences that candidate has. It is comprised of lists of skill sets.

But it's wrong.

You see, the **real** purpose of a Functional résumé is to **hide** from recruiters what the applicant lacks. It obscures inexperience, gaps in employment, a 'jumpy' applicant who changes jobs often, career path tangents, and other possible challenges for the application. Recruiters hate to read them because they usually know what the person is trying to hide. They know all the tricks and have no patience for the résumé that tries to sneak something past them!

I worked with one top pharmaceutical company and their recruiter refused to short-list a candidate I had submitted who was a great fit just because they hid a large gap in their experience behind a Functional format. His explanation was that that kind of dishonesty isn't a corporate fit for the company.

Harsh? Yes, but it happens. The good news is that it won't happen to you.

RÉSUMÉ SUCCESS 600 SURVEY HIGHLIGHT

Over 90% of recruiters from top companies prefer the *Reverse Chronological* format to *any* other format.

One Alternative

There are people who are traditionally pushed towards the Functional format because they aren't typical applicants. New grads who have no real career experience, those leaving the military looking for their first civilian job, people who are returning to the workforce after a lengthy absence, and so on. Since we know now that the RC is the ideal format, it's important not to veer far from this form.

The answer is the **Hybrid** résumé, sometimes called the **Combination** résumé. It is an amalgam of Reverse Chronological and Functional formats. It accents skill sets because of lack of experience but doesn't disrespect the recruiter by trying to hide the job seeker's situation. It manages to successfully retain the overall flow and readability of a RC formatted résumé.

The True Curriculum Vitae

The only other format that you may need to know about is the true **Curriculum Vitae,** Latin for *'the course of one's life'*. This résumé can be in excess of ten or even twenty pages and is reserved for the scientific, academic, and medical professionals.

Reserved for academics and intellectuals striving for roles in competitive areas of specialization, the CV is a weighty, detailed document. Scientists, professors, students, and medical professionals have the need to put together a full CV. No one else needs to create one, or should even try!

If your experience is very lean, even a 2 page CV can work, but I have seen them up to 15 pages and tightly edited. The key differences between a CV and a traditional résumé are that the CV candidate needs a fuller range of included sections that highlight multiple areas of development. Licensure, Certification, Teaching Appointments, Training, information on their PHD dissertation, Honors, Awards, Achievements, Research Experience, Publications, Presentations, Projects, Affiliations, Credentials, Recommendations, will all be a part of a quality CV.

The key to a successful CV is understanding that recruiters interested in this type of professional **want** to see the minutia, they need to see every significant thing you bring to the table. Whereas a regular résumé reviewer looks for a synopsis, a CV reviewer wants to learn about everything you have learned, taught, experimented with, proven, published, and presented.

Due to my attempt at brevity here the lengthy CV format cannot be covered in depth. However, should you have any questions about that style, feel free to contact me at **david@davidjgardner.com** and I will provide you with the information you need!

Let's Get Started!

I know by now you're chomping at the bit, eager to get to the real deal…so let's start building!

Software

Unless you've just been found frozen in a glacier, you use a computer to do pretty well everything. Until recently there were a variety of software programs that were commonly used for word processing. The extension attached to the end of the saved document would reflect your file type and your software. If you used WordPerfect, a document would be saved as a **wpd** file, whereas if you used Word for Windows, it would be a **doc** file. As mentioned, many résumé books even three years ago suggested that you also save your résumé in **ascii** or **rtf** or **'rich text format'** file so that the company software could read, reproduce, scan, and use the content easily.

The good news for technophobes is that with the alignment of platforms and new compatibility of programs, the need for traditional **ascii** or **rtf** formatted résumés has disappeared. Also, WordPerfect has diminished in popularity and MS Word has become a universal standard in word processing. Further good news came with the availability of MS Office for Macs, so virtually everyone can use Word to compose their résumé. You should, too.

Another format used to submit résumés is the **pdf** format. Also called **'portable document format'**, the pdf was originally a proprietary format developed by Adobe Systems in the early 1990's. Imagine it to be like a photograph of your résumé rather than an editable document. So long as your computer has Adobe Acrobat installed, it can view a pdf document. The advantage of a pdf is that it's very **wysiwyg,** or *'what you see is what you get'*. As a fixed image file, when you send it there is no chance that it will come out differently than the way you sent it. If it looks perfect on your side, you save it as a pdf file and nothing will misalign it, move pagination, or shift margins as can sometimes be the case with regular documents. The downside of pdf is that unless one has Adobe Professional or a specific conversion program, it's very challenging to manipulate the information in it. The recruiter will sometimes want to make electronic notes directly on your résumé for themselves or the hiring manager. More importantly, some Applicant Tracking Systems have problems importing pdf files to its database, and you want to make it easy, not difficult.

I prefer email doc files - database friendly. If I have to scan your résumé into a format to add it to my database, chances are I will have my administrator do it and never read it myself—PDF = Lost in cyberspace!
Jacqui Gallagher—Sr. Recruiter, David Aplin Recruiting

If you don't have access to Word, save the résumé in what format you can, and later have a friend or colleague convert it for you.

> Create your résumé in Word and save the file as a 'doc' file. On the Mac computer you have the option of saving the file as a superior 'docx' file, but resist the urge to do so...some recruiters will not be able to read it, or it may open formatted poorly. Stick with the standard doc and you will be fine.

INSIDER SECRET

From here on this chapter will lead you through the Résumé Success formatting rules to remember and steps to build your own Master Résumé Template. With your Master Résumé saved you will be able to easily tailor specifically targeted résumés for every role you deem worthy of applying for.

STEP 3a: Set up your Master Résumé Template file

Open a new document in Word, and save this file as **'master_resume_template.doc'** and make sure the file is saved somewhere handy as you'll be using it to build your résumé framework as we move forward this chapter. You needn't include your name or profession in the file title, since this will be used for your own reference as a template whenever you need to start from scratch to build a résumé.

RÉSUMÉ SUCCESS 600 SURVEY HIGHLIGHT

84% of agency recruiters prefer doc files over any other format
16% accept either doc OR pdf

67% of corporate recruiters prefer doc format
3% prefer docx
50% accept pdf or doc
11% would accept, but not prefer, wpd
6% would accept txt format (as in Wordpad).

Paper

Older books often spend a good deal of time reviewing the types of paper that should be used when preparing a résumé. The idea is that since you will be mailing it out to each prospective employer or carrying it in to each interview, the paper selection is important.

We've already gone over the transition away from the mailing and faxing of résumés to the ubiquitous e-submission via the Internet. Does this, then, mean that the paper résumé has gone the way of the dodo?

Not necessarily.

There remain several useful purposes for the paper résumé. When you go to interview, it's always a good idea to bring a notepad, pen, and a copy of your résumé for yourself and each interviewer. While not common, it is occasionally the case that a recruiter, harried by innumerable tasks tugging at their schedule, may herd you into a meeting room for interview having forgotten to print off your résumé. What a great show of initiative it will be when you hand them a crisp, attractive copy for them to make notes on! Even if they **don't** need it, mentioning that you brought one for them shows forethought and they'll appreciate it. Remember, in an interview the printed résumé remains essential. Also, if you attend a job fair, which we'll go over in the Submission chapter, you will need a healthy number of printed résumés to hand to recruiters there.

While the need for a paper résumé still exists, its relegation to secondary importance as the medium for initial review of your experience means that vast explanations of color, weight, and watermarking of paper are no longer very necessary.

Keep it simple, neat, and professional. When considering color, a clean white, cream, ivory, eggshell, or light grey are fine. White is best. Resist the temptation to use flashy color paper to get attention. Even if you are a marketing professional used to using creative techniques to get your message across, remember that the résumé gatekeeper, the recruiter you will hand it to in interview may not be amused by your fluorescent yellow résumé.

Exquisite papers with silk, potpourri, flowers or whatever screened into the paper are a poor choice. Simple can be elegant and professional.

When you go to shop for paper for your résumé, you'll likely want a better quality than the draft paper you use for most home printing jobs, but no need to go overboard. Look for paper weight between 20 and 25 pound stock, standard or watermarked bond paper. Oh, and only print on one side of the paper.

That's really all you need to know about paper.

Formatting for Success: The Basics

Font Type

What were once called **typefaces** are now almost universally known as **fonts.** In truth, the name of what we now call a font is actually still a typeface, and it's the size and variety of the typeface that indicates the font. Ariel is a typeface, but Ariel Bold 10pt is a font. These are the family of characters used in printed (electronic, paper, or otherwise) that give a document a certain feel or personality.

There are two main types, *serif* and **sans serif.** Serif fonts have little horizontal strokes called serifs at bottom of each character, giving them a more professional, traditional feel.

Sans serif fonts, meaning 'without serif', like Ariel, removes the serif lines for a cleaner, more modern feel like the majority of text in this book.

When choosing a font for your résumé, it's safest to be conservative. Imagine a recruiter trying to take you seriously if you submitted your résumé in a non-traditional font such as:

Blackoak, Curlz MT, **Hobo, Braggadocio, ROSEWOOD ST, or STENCIL STD.**

Fun, wow!! Bring out the dancing bears!…but no job for you.

Also, non-traditional fonts often translate poorly as they are added to recruiter databases, ATS, operating systems, programs, and web portals. Not all computer systems are able to support all font types. Better safe than garbled!

I have seen excellent résumés in both serif and sans serif format. Generally, more seasoned professionals with maturity and higher up the corporate ladder almost exclusively use the serif font, and younger, more inexperienced use either serif or sans serif. Default to serif if you try both and aren't sure which to use.

Some examples of quality serif fonts are: Times New Roman, Cambria, Garamond, Century, Bookman Old Style, and Goudy Old Style.

Helvetica, **Arial**, and **Verdana** are examples of well-used sans serif fonts.

INSIDER SECRET

Don't mix font types on your résumé; stick with just one. Multiple fonts look unprofessional and recruiters will think you just haven't paid attention to detail. Consistency is quality.

While **bold**, *italics,* and underline use have their place on a résumé, don't overdo it! Too much can result in a visual imbalance and general sense of clutter that you don't want.

ALSO, WHILE UPPERCASE LETTERS CALL ATTENTION TO THEM-SELVES, IT'S LIKE YOU'RE YELLING AT THE RECRUITER AND THAT'S JUST NOT SMART!

Use full upper case words sparingly. In fact, if you decide to cut them out entirely your résumé will not suffer.

Keep it simple. Keep it legible. Ensure that it is black type on white paper, not fancy colors or fonts!
Peter Shenfield—Recruiting Consultant, Bayer

Font Size

Size your fonts at the default 12 points as you work. If you find that your résumé is growing too long, change the whole body to 11 and see if it remains easily readable. 10–12 point fonts are acceptable, but with an aging population creating possible visibility issues it's safer to use the 12 pt for readability if possible. If you feel the need to move down to 9 point to fit in your content…you need to edit; 10 is the smallest you should go.

As you see from the examples the heading is a larger font, as is the Contact Information and other headings. Generally use this rule: Your name will be largest, followed by the section headings and Contact Information, then subheadings. The rest should be set at one standard size. You can see the breakdown as follows, and the template created also bears out this consistency.

NAME (16)
Heading (14)
Subheading (12)

Content (10)

When you are resizing your résumé for fit, if you should need to change the size of your font hierarchy up or down, retain their ratios to each other. Don't shrink your name to smaller than the section titles, for example.

Bullets

Bullet lists are an important format ingredient to include in your successful résumé, but again, do not mix! You may choose not to use the identical bullet form for every instance on your résumé, but keep them in the same family. If you start with a box bullet, you can use another form of box bullet, but don't switch to a checkmark or circular bullet form mid résumé.

- This is a circle bullet
  - This is a 2nd generation circle bullet, and it can complement the first
    - Don't use a square if you've begun with circles

Flushed

The alignment of your résumé content is another aspect that requires some consideration. **Flush left,** or **ragged right** alignment as it's sometimes called, refers to a document where there is a clean line on the left side of the page, but on the right side it is uneven. The challenge with this alignment is that the right side, some people feel, seems unkempt and in disorder; something you may choose to avoid on your résumé.

The alternative is the justification alignment, like the majority of this book, wherein the text is cleanly cut on both the left and right side, giving a neater appearance. The challenge with this alignment is that the program will stretch out the text to make sure it fits neatly and if you have a few longer words it can look odd.

If the résumé were a document where full, flowing sentences led to paragraphs, justified margins would work. But the best current-day résumés are powerful, point form pieces, with no paragraphs, and no sentences by the traditional definition. Stick with ragged right.

Margins

When you open up a new blank document in your word processing program, it automatically sets the margins, or distances from the top, bottom, left, and right side of the page that print will appear. Just leave the default settings as they are when building your résumé. Should you have too much information or not enough to fit attractively on the page, we will go over a few techniques to change that in Chapter 6.

White Space

When the importance of an excellent résumé is fully grasped, many job seekers are paralyzed by uncertainty as they struggle to decide what to include, and how much. Some people crowd their résumé with everything they've done from babysitting in high school to bringing the charcoal to the annual company picnic. They shrink the fonts, enlarge the margins, and create a very busy-looking résumé, filled with unnecessary information. They marvel at it, feeling more is better.

It's not.

White space on a résumé is very attractive to a reader. If done properly, it doesn't lead to a sense that you don't have enough experience to fill the page, but rather that you are efficient in your use of that experience and want to help the recruiter through a clean, clear, easy-to-read paper. As we will learn in the next chapter, if you choose the most powerful and appropriate words, you can actually say more with less language and clutter. Font size, margins, spacing, organization, all contribute to creating white space on a résumé.

Line Spacing

Adjusting the line spacing, or gap between one line and the next, can be a very effective tool in adding more content without compromising white space or balance. Regardless of what spacing you choose for your résumé, make sure it is consistent! If you leave a 4-point gap in between Responsibilities and the next section, then do it in each part of the résumé. Simply put your cursor on the space between written lines and check your font dialog box for what size font that line is set at, then change as necessary.

Tabs

Tabs move your content to the right by increments and are used to inset groups of information, displaying neater organization and differentiating it from other areas. Use them, but again, sparingly. You don't want information listed in 5 staggered tabs or it will get confusing for your reader and take the balance away. Also, be careful, as when you save/email/populate a web portal, sometimes the tabs shift awkwardly.

Page Count

There was a time, hardly a generation ago that had job seekers forced to confine their entire professional experience to just **one** page. Those were the days when many employees worked very few jobs in their life. They stuck it out with one employer for 10, 20, even 30 years or more. Alas, life is more complicated now…with the current multi-job and even multi-career experience that most applicants bring to the table, it's impossible to appropriately convey your employment with a one-pager.

This expansion of roles, experiences, and responsibilities led employers in the 1980's to embrace the two-page résumé. Here was a format that could readily reflect all that an applicant had to share, and all a recruiter wanted to read. Fewer and fewer one-pagers appeared. Nowadays the only one-page résumés we see come from new grads that have no experience, and yet even some of these can manage two after including volunteer work, courses, and listed personal references!

Surprisingly, in recent years there has been an appearance and rising acceptance of the **three-page** résumé. With the further increase in job and career changes, increased number of required sections, use of electronic submission, and the formatting challenges that can come from these changes, many recruiters have no issue with reading a three-pager.

Try not to make it longer than 4 pages because its purpose is to provide the highlights of your experience and education and technical skills to do the job.
Carla Spadafora— HR Analyst, Enbridge, Canada

If you have the relevant experience to fill it out well, a three-page résumé can be a powerful thing, including everything you need without worrying about nipping and tucking margins, spacing, and fonts to get it all to fit. **However, do not use a three-pager if you can readily edit down to two pages.** A loose three-page résumé with extra fluff, irrelevant information, and poorly edited content can actually do more damage than good.

Finally, do not submit a résumé that provides two full pages, then spills a few lines onto a third page. Formatting inconsistencies with browsers, programs, and portals increase the likelihood of this, so email yourself and also a colleague (who may have a different program version than you) a copy of your résumé to check that it will open cleanly in e-format.

Résumé Sections

Let's go into a detailed, top to bottom tour of the Reverse Chronological résumé. This specific layout of the format comes directly from the research, interviews, and experience of the **Résumé Success 600** group. This is precisely how recruiters want to see your résumé. If you meet a recruiter who says otherwise, they are an exception, and not the rule.

As we move through the structure, we'll be building your ultimate template. It is the framework around which we will wrap compelling Content next chapter to create your Master Résumé. You may want to read the next few chapters by your computer so that you can work along with each step.

Reverse Chronological Résumé Sections:
'Must Have' Sections

Contact Information

Your Contact Information is the first section of the résumé, right at the top, and it's best centered. The purpose of this section is to let the recruiter know your name and how to get ahold of you. This may seem foolishly simple, but you would be surprised at how many people neglect to use this section effectively.

NAME: Your name goes first and set in the largest font on your résumé. Remember, it's **your brand** that's being sold here, so let them know who you are. If your name is the same size as your address then it feels like a diminishment of your importance. It is a recruiting fact that a large, clear name is more apt to leave a stronger impression than a small one. Just don't get carried away.

Many people choose to embolden their name at the top, further drawing attention to it. This works very well, so try it.

When recording your name, make sure that you use the name that you would like to be referred to as, not necessarily your full name. If your name is Robert and you list your name as Bob, then the recruiter will follow your protocol and call you Bob. If you write Robert, they will call you Robert. If you correct them in interview, it could be uncomfortable and unnecessary.

If you have a lengthy name, or if your name may be a mouthful for a recruiter, consider using your nickname. While they will never discriminate based upon your name, you want to make their lives as easy as possible. I had a great candidate named Xiao-Niao. I had no idea how to pronounce it and it was embarrassing for me...it was also embarrassing for my client and Xiao-Niao herself. After chatting with her, she told me her English name was Lisa. Why didn't she say so!? We changed it on her résumé and the issue was resolved.

Do **not** use your nickname if it's **just** a nickname. Justin 'Mad Dog' Campbell at the top of your résumé is not professional and may well get your résumé into the garbage without another glance.

Don't mess around with your last name in any situation.

If you possess a professional designation, make sure it is prominently displayed beside your name:

David J. Gardner MBA PhD CA

Many hiring managers will be flexible on some job description criteria, but not designation. If they tell a recruiter that they want a Chartered Accountant (CA), you don't want them to have to dig through your résumé to discover if you are designated.

If you went to university and got a degree, you may consider putting this beside your name. There are differing schools of thought on this practice.

David J. Gardner Hons. BA English Specialist, B.Ed.

A good rule of thumb is that if you **know** that it will be an advantage to have it there, add it. For example, a junior level accounting professional who has not yet earned a designation in the field, but who has a Bachelor of Commerce or Economics degree may list it:

David J. Gardner B.Comm

If you were vying for an Accounting Manager position, a B.Comm degree wouldn't be relevant, as they would assume you are designated and your undergraduate degree would be less important.

If you are enrolled in course work but have yet to graduate, **never** include that designation or degree beside your name; you haven't earned it yet. We'll cover where this goes later on.

ADDRESS: Immediately following your name comes your address. Take one or two lines for this important piece of contact information. If you can't comfortably list your full postal address on one line, feel free to use two. Avoid extending your address to a 3rd line, as there are other pieces of information to add and you don't want your Contact Information section to be too long.

Be accurate. If you live at unit 1-b, then state that. Ensure it is your correct mailing address in full. You wouldn't want a company preparing an offer letter to courier to you and being without a proper address, would you? Some candidates seem to limit their address to city name and country, or leave it out entirely due to a perceived privacy issue, or because they don't want to be discounted if they live too far from the company location. Recruiters may assume they have something to hide.

PHONE NUMBER: Okay, this is a sore spot for a lot of recruiters. If you include a phone number on your résumé, you **want** a recruiter to call it, right? If so, you must make it easy for them!! Recruiters will most often call and not mail or email you first. The submission of your résumé or application is all the permission they need to pick up the phone and reach out to you if they deem you a good potential fit. Far too often the recruiter encounters an incorrect phone number, a garbled or inappropriate message box greeting, or a person who answers and has no idea where the applicant is. Many times a recruiter's call is answered by a candidate who is at work and around colleagues or employers, leading to an awkward one-sided conversation.

Use one number if you can. It should be a number that has a clear and polite voicemail message indicating that you will call back within, ideally a few hours or less. You can list more than one phone number if your first number isn't readily accessible at all times. If you list others, make sure you can take calls there or retrieve the messages readily. Most common are: Cell, Home, and Business, in order of prevalence. We'll cover this topic in greater detail in Chapter 8.

> *It's becoming more and more common that people are leaving their address off their résumé. It can be a huge factor in whether or not I consider you for a position. Put it on!*
>
> Nicole Bradfield—Recruitment Consultant, Placement Group

INSIDER SECRET

Don't bother right aligning, splitting, or boxing your contact information. You may feel it makes the résumé more professional or provide more panache, but it's just distracting. Keep it simple!

EMAIL: Use the newly created, job-search specific email address we created in Chapter 2. Clearly designed, this tag will show a recruiter you are organized and professional.

Name, address, phone number(s), email address, and that's it. Fax numbers are largely obsolete, pagers are all but history, and newer trends, such as social networking website links are not to be used. We'll discuss these in the chapter on Submission.

STEP 3b: Create the Contact Information section

Open your résumé template document, and with the alignment set to Centre, use the above information to complete your Contact Information Section. It should look something like this:

NAME
Street address, City, State/Province, zip/postal code
Phone: xxx-xxx-xxxx
Email

The name is set at 16 point, emboldened. Once you're finished this section, move down to the next line, return the alignment to **left,** and save the file. The following steps will involve formatting your résumé without including actual content. As mentioned, we will populate it in the next chapters.

Note that we don't actually type the section title 'Contact Information' on the résumé…self-evident. We do, however, include titles for all other sections, and most subsections.

Core Competencies

A valuable lead in to your résumé beneath Contact Information is the Core Competencies section in its many forms and aliases. It's also known as the **Professional Profile, Career Synopsis, Summary of Qualifications, Key Features, Performance Profile, Career Highlights, Skills Summary,** and a multitude of other variations and permutations. Core Competencies or Professional Profile is preferred, but so long as the heading describes well the list contained below, you can call it what you will.

This section is an important one, representing a distillation of everything you bring to the table professionally. If your résumé is your career in a few pages, this section is your résumé in 6–8 bullet points. This is where we take the specific achievements and skills developed in the full résumé and group them together, with impressive cumulative results. Think of it as the marquee at a movie theatre; its job is to show, in byte form, the most impressive you, to attract people to enter the theatre and take a closer look at the film that is your career, or a recruiter to take the time to read what follows thoroughly. As the résumé gatekeeper takes their initial five second glance at your résumé, scanning this section is usually the first stop…so it'd better be good or they may well pass you by without reading further.

A strong résumé will include 6–8 bulleted points here, ideally 6. More than this and you risk diluting your brand and lessening the impact. It will feel to a recruiter like you're trying to be that jack-of-all trades. No sentences here. Advantages of a strong Core Competencies section are:

- By not specifically naming one job title here, and instead listing competence areas with strong details, you qualify yourself for multiple roles within an organization without being limited to one.

- A set of outstanding quantifiable experiences synopsized here is the first and most powerful area of impact, helping you show a recruiter not what you want from them, but rather what you can do for them.

- This section and the details included will further increase the likelihood of the bots that search engines use to find people with a relevant skill set. We may have nixed a keyword section, but not the value of keywords!

- The more overall experience you have, the more potent this section will be as a summary of all you bring to the table.

- The general sections not specifically outlined in a traditional Reverse Chronological résumé and most often the key of a Functional résumé can be safely, and impressively, expressed here, adding to the RC's potency

- This section will include both 'hard' skills, which are direct work and profession related sections, and 'soft skills', which are more behavioral, such as people management and the like, and equally important in your overall professional pedigree. We well drill down the details of this section in the next chapter.

> *The Profile or Core Competencies tells me how well you know yourself and how capable you are of achieving your goals. I have an idea how good the entire résumé is (and the person) by just the first 6 lines.*
>
> Chris Kershaw— Managing Director, Miramas.

STEP 3c: Create the Core Competencies section

Beneath your Contact Information, create the above section as it appears. The Heading 'Core Competencies' (or whichever you choose) is set to 14-point font size, and the points, which will be consistent as the smallest and most common in the résumé, is 10-point. Again, we use Garamond. You may choose to underline it if you prefer.

Core Competencies

Key strength

Key strength

Key strength

Key strength

Key strength

Key strength

Key strength

Perfect! Now let's move on.

Professional Experience

The Experience section of your résumé is the real meat and potatoes of your work history. In this section we will use the detailed experiential highlights of your career we drew out last chapter. Here you will list your positions held with company details and responsibilities for each, beginning with the most recent or current employer first. The Professional

Experience will take up the majority of space on your résumé. Let's break down the formatting for this section, in order of appearance:

Section Title: **Professional Experience** should be the same font and same size as the **Core Competencies** section header.

Job Title: In most situations, the first thing you will add will be your most recent job title. Remember that recruiters are looking for your employment relevance to the job description they are working on, so they want to see the comparability of your title with their search.

Company Name: Following this, separated by a comma, you will enter the name of the company you last worked. We have found that small caps (LIKE THIS!) work well for the names of companies. Enter the name in full, and, if it was acquired by another company, record the new name, and in brackets 'Formerly ___'.

> **NOTE**: there are some situations where it will be not only permissible but actually to your advantage to reverse job title and company name. If the company you worked for is more important than your title in a submission for a role, then by all means, put the company first. More on this later in the chapter.

Location: Recruiters will want to know where your company was, and you can't fool them. I had a candidate who had worked for PepsiCo and Microsoft, and proudly displayed this on his résumé. The assumption, of course, was that this was domestic employment as these are North American employers. I asked which state or province they were in, and was told **Abu Dhabi.** Of course there's nothing wrong with Abu Dhabi, and it **may** not preclude someone from moving to an interview…sometimes companies are very open to international movement. However, knowing it might be an issue and leaving it off to sneak in *never* works. A recruiter will spot it and be put off by the ploy.

Dates of Employment: On the same line as the position title, company name, and location, on the right margin you will list the dates of employment. Use the tab key to do this and not the space bar, as you will want to put other dates in the identical vertical line later on. So this section, with the others before it, will look like this:

NAME

Street address, City, State/Province, zip/postal code
Phone: xxx-xxx-xxxx
Email

Core Competencies

Key strength
Key strength
Key strength
Key strength
Key strength
Key strength

Professional Experience

Job title, COMPANY, Location   July '04–Oct. '05

(This page is an actual 8.5 x 11 paper reduced 69% to fit the text area of this book.)

INSIDER SECRET

Notice that the dates on the last three roles include *month,* even if abbreviated. (Rules on punctuation will be explained in the next chapter). This is important. If you leave out months, recruiters may think you are trying to hide gaps in your résumé. In many instances that's exactly what people are trying to do. Don't let yourself fall into this trap. Be honest; remember, recruiters are people like you and will understand. If you can fill the entire résumé with months, it adds continuity and shows good organization. However, if you can't recall the months for positions beyond the most recent three, or 10–12 years, then you can go with the year only.

STEP 3d: Create the Professional Experience section

Enter the above title, company, and work date information onto your résumé. The next several steps will flesh out this principal area.

Company Synopsis: Under the above line, write a short blurb about the company. Just as with the Contact Information section, you needn't entitle it, just include the contents. An often-neglected ingredient in a successful résumé, this section shows the recruiter important information about the company you worked at.

In your Master Résumé Template, simply enter the following. We'll bring it together later:

Industry, product, size, revenues, scope, sector, placement

STEP 3e: Create the Company Synopsis section

Enter the above content to your template and save it. It should appear similar to this:

NAME

Street address, City, State/Province, zip/postal code
Phone: xxx-xxx-xxxx
Email

Core Competencies

Key strength
Key strength
Key strength
Key strength
Key strength
Key strength

Professional Experience

Job title, COMPANY, Location   July '04–Oct. '05
Industry, product, size, revenues, scope, sector, placement

As noted in the last chapter, 92% of recruiters appreciate reading this subsection and less than 5% use it.

RESPONSIBILITIES: Beneath the Company Synopsis, and in bullet form, you will list the duties or key deliverables of your role we created last chapter. This is an important list because while the duties of someone with your position title might be similar to another, you can never assume it's identical. The title of 'Intermediate Programmer' at one company can come with strikingly different responsibilities depending upon many different factors. In this section you will list the responsibilities required of you on a daily, monthly, quarterly, and annual basis, along with project work that is a part of your role. This part or your résumé is the 'What you did' area, and we want it to be an excellent match for the job descriptions that you printed out earlier. Again, we will populate this section in the next two chapters!

STEP 3f: Create the Responsibilities section

Create 8–10 Bullet points in one column as below. You needn't input your personal information yet, just note at each bullet point **'Responsibility'.**

ACCOMPLISHMENTS: This section, more than any other on your résumé is where a recruiter can easily fall in love with your background. Whereas the Responsibilities section will list what you were expected to do and did, the Accomplishments section shows **how well you did it, and what you did that was above and beyond the call.** When **agency** recruiters were asked about ingredients that were essential to a **great** résumé, 100% agreed that the Accomplishments section needed to be there! Nine out of ten **corporate** recruiters also love to see an Accomplishment section, too!

RÉSUMÉ SUCCESS 600 SURVEY HIGHLIGHT

91% of all recruiters LOVE to see the Accomplishment section on a résumé, and yet less than 19% of applicants include it and less than 5% do it effectively!

This section will differentiate you from everyone else. While others in your position would have had the same responsibilities, **only you** have achieved results in your Accomplishment section. In this section you will detail **how you made money, saved money, or introduced/improved a process.** If you submit your résumé to a posting looking for a Sr. Financial Analyst, there will likely be 50 or more other Sr. Financial Analysts applying for the same position. If only you had the insight to include a powerful Accomplishments section, it will clearly set you apart!

We include it here at the end of the duties for that position. Some people add a whole section entitled Achievements or Accomplishments at the end of their résumé, or even the very beginning. Some résumé preparers advise to do this. This is a **mistake,** as the recruiter wants to see your impact in **each** role, so that they can evaluate your accomplishments within each work situation, giving them context.

RÉSUMÉ SUCCESS 600 SURVEY HIGHLIGHT

More than 75% of all recruiters want to see the Accomplishments section below the Responsibilities list for that position and not in its own section elsewhere on a résumé.

STEP 3g: Create the Accomplishments section

Add a subheading 'Accomplishments' under the last responsibility on your template, with 3 bulleted points. This is a subheading under Professional Experience, so it takes a smaller font size.

Here is one of the most powerful statements in this book: *EVERY employer wants to hire someone who saved money, made money, or improved or introduced a process.* When your résumé reflects this, recruiters will take notice.

INSIDER SECRET

Professional Experience
Job title, COMPANY, Location   July '04–Oct. '05
 Industry, product, size, revenues, scope, sector, placement

Responsibilities:

- Responsibility
- Responsibility
- Responsibility
- Responsibility
- Responsibility
- Responsibility
- Responsibility

Accomplishments:

- Saved money/made money/process/awards/recognition
- Saved money/made money/process/awards/recognition
- Saved money/made money/process/awards/recognition

You will notice that the section headings are in emboldened and underlined, the position titles are emboldened, company name is small caps and underlined, and the Company Synopsis is italicized. Bullets for Responsibilities are not indented to provide more room to their right, and Accomplishments are indented slightly with a variant bullet type within the same round family. By mixing up the font formatting we can draw attention to individual details without sacrificing readability. Many people instead elect to change font types, which is distracting for a reader and reduces flow.

I want to see Accomplishments … and I want to see them beneath Responsibilities at each role so I know where they did it.
Natasha Gill—Recruiter, Rogers Communications.

How Many Jobs?

You will repeat the Responsibilities and Accomplishments section for each of your last three roles. In positions you list older than that, you can consolidate the Responsibilities to fewer bullet points. Your most recent positions are your most relevant ones, and so they will be prominent. Older ones should not be ignored, but packaged more tightly.

How Far Back?

20 years is a reasonable length of time to have represented on your résumé. However, there are exceptions. If you are new enough to the workforce that you don't have that length of career history, just use what you do have and don't worry; your current roles are most important. If you have more than 20–25 years experience, you can cut your oldest experience, or simply list the position, company, and tenure. You want consistency, so rather than cut piecemeal experience out over your entire career to show strength in one area your job search requires, remove the oldest and show the smooth transitions since that time.

STEP 3h: Duplicate sections throughout résumé template

Duplicate the Responsibilities and Accomplishments section several times, with the final two being smaller in content. Save your template.

Your Template should now look something like this:

NAME

Street address, City, State/Province, zip/postal code
Phone: xxx-xxx-xxxx
Email

Core Competencies

Key strength
Key strength
Key strength
Key strength
Key strength
Key strength

Professional Experience

Job title, COMPANY, Location mo/yr–mo/yr

Industry, product, size, revenues, scope, sector, placement

Responsibilities:

- Responsibility
- Responsibility
- Responsibility
- Responsibility
- Responsibility
- Responsibility
- Responsibility

Accomplishments:

- Saved money/made money/process/awards/recognition
- Saved money/made money/process/awards/recognition
- Saved money/made money/process/awards/recognition

Job title, COMPANY, Location mo/yr–mo/yr

Industry, product, size, revenues, scope, sector, placement

Responsibilities:

- Responsibility
- Responsibility
- Responsibility
- Responsibility
- Responsibility
- Responsibility
- Responsibility

Accomplishments:

- Saved money/made money/process/awards/recognition
- Saved money/made money/process/awards/recognition
- Saved money/made money/process/awards/recognition

(continued)

Job title, Company, Location   mo/yr–mo/yr
Industry, product, size, revenues, scope, sector, placement

Responsibilities:
- Responsibility
- Responsibility
- Responsibility
- Responsibility
- Responsibility
- Responsibility
- Responsibility

Accomplishments:
- Saved money/made money/process/awards/recognition
- Saved money/made money/process/awards/recognition
- Saved money/made money/process/awards/recognition

Ahhh, that looks **outstanding!** We love to receive résumés with this balance, attractiveness, organization…like it was designed specifically to help me help you!

What About Promotions?

Promotions show a recruiter that you have the ability to grow within an organization. They reflect your development to a point whereat management deems you will contribute more at a high level. Remember, many companies could 'keep you down' if you are on top of your game at your current level; it's not your **right** to be promoted. Companies promote proven successes, and so if you have been promoted, even if the role falls somewhat outside your current focus, make sure your résumé reflects this. Recruiters are wary of someone below senior management who has spent 10 years in the same role without movement or promotion. They will wonder what the issue is; lack of ambition? Confidence? Ability? Promotions should be included. In fact, some extra care should be taken to have attention drawn to them. While some roles such as teachers are not promotion-based, the bulk of corporate and industry positions are, and so inclusion of promotion is worthwhile. Find below an example of expressing a promotion:

Professional Experience

H&N FOODS INTERNATIONAL, TORONTO, Ontario
2nd largest produce distributor in North America, with 35 warehouses, 2,300 employees, and net annual sales over $389M

Sales Manager *(Promotion)*   **June 2005–Present**

Responsibilities:
- Responsibility
- Responsibility
- Responsibility
- Responsibility
- Responsibility
- Responsibility
- Responsibility

Accomplishments:
- ◦ Saved money/made money/process/awards/recognition
- ◦ Saved money/made money/process/awards/recognition
- ◦ Saved money/made money/process/awards/recognition

Sales Representative   **April 2004–June 2005**

Responsibilities:
- Responsibility
- Responsibility
- Responsibility
- Responsibility
- Responsibility
- Responsibility
- Responsibility

Accomplishments:
- ◦ Saved money/made money/process/awards/recognition
- ◦ Saved money/made money/process/awards/recognition
- ◦ Saved money/made money/process/awards/recognition

In this example, the position title has been taken from the first line and instead we begin with the company name. We do this because when there are promotions to list, the company becomes as a headline, and each position within the company acts as a subheading. A small space can separate the company information with the positions. You see how the company becomes a master heading but the positions themselves retain the feeling of importance. Also, you see we listed 'Promotion' beside the title. The recruiter will make the assumption that you were promoted but it's a powerful word and has a positive non-conscious impact on a recruiter. We all want to hire people who a good enough to be promoted!

INSIDER SECRET In most situations it's best to list your position title first, then the company you worked at next on your résumé. *However,* if you worked for an industry leader, a company that will certainly impress a recruiter due to a relevant aspect of their business, it can pay to *reverse* the two and put the company name first. Be consistent throughout the résumé.

EDUCATION: The final 'Must Have' section on your résumé is the Education section. In almost every case your work experience will be more relevant than your education to an employer so it goes first.

There are exceptional instances where your education might be listed **before** your experience. If your education is more relevant than your experience for the job you are considering, earlier listing may help. However, if a requirement for education resulting in a designation or certification is foremost, its inclusion beside your name at the top of the résumé often removes this need.

Some people list the Education first if they returned to school to get a designation or degree. While an advanced degree or professional designation is listed beside your name in Contact Information, some designations are perceived to be somewhat time sensitive. A CPA or CGA in 2010 may be seen to have more current information and qualification than a similar designation from 1993, for example, even if ongoing professional development courses largely remove this obstacle. For this reason you may choose to list this above the Experience section.

If you have any doubts, put it after your Professional Experience. It's your safest bet.

List your Education in reverse chronological order as you did with your professional experience. Name the school, the location, the degree/diploma attained, and year of graduation. It will look something like this:

University of Manitoba, Winnipeg, MB
Bachelor of Education Degree—B.Ed., K-12   1996

York University, Toronto, ON
Bachelor of Arts Degree—B.A., English Major   1993

We included both the long and abbreviated form of the degree so that recruiters won't miss you if they use keyword searches. If your major is relevant to the role you are applying to, you can list that as well.

If you didn't complete your degree or diploma, you should record that as 'courses taken' as shown below.

Ryerson University, Toronto, ON
Courses taken in Accounting towards
    Chartered Accountant designation.   2006

Don't leave it off just because you didn't finish, as your coursework will certainly help in your qualification! If you are currently enrolled in coursework toward a designation, degree, diploma or similarly relevant educational goal, make sure you include it in this section.

If you have a post-secondary degree or college diploma, you can leave off your high school information. The exception is that if the role you are applying for is an entry level one that specifically asks for a high school credentials, include it.

In the rare case that you have no post-secondary education **and** you are a seasoned worker, you can leave off Education entirely. Also, if you are a new entrant to the workforce and did not complete high school, it's best to leave off the Education section.

The widely-accepted belief that education helps to sell your ability is quite true. If there are two people with similar skills and background, a company will often choose the one with the better educational pedigree. There are some positions, sales roles, for example, that stress a skill and mindset and do not necessarily push for post-secondary education. These are in the minority, however. For this reason it's **always** a good idea to complete your education if you've neglected it, at any age, or further your existing credentials if you can afford the tuition and time.

If you have a degree or diploma from a foreign school, you should get it evaluated for equivalency. You cannot assume that your foreign degree has the same clout in North America, so it's best to have a professional institution provide you proof of equivalence. More than this, many universities will allow you to take any courses you are missing and issue you a degree from their school. Educational levels are different all over the world and so are the expectations of post-secondary schools!

I once had a woman with a Bachelors Degree from a South American college apply to a position I posted. Her overall experience and résumé was strong, so I interviewed her, shortlisted her, and sent her to my client, a top company. The client liked her and asked about her education. The applicant feigned naïveté but said that it was the equivalent of a genuine Bachelors Degree. I did some digging, and you have to assume that at some point SOMEONE will check, and found out that this 'college' was actually a high school. Both the client and I dropped this candidate and I wouldn't represent her again. Not because of the education, but rather, the dishonesty.

*Another candidate came from a foreign country with seemingly advanced accounting credentials. After months of lukewarm response in the job market, I suggested that he increase his legitimacy in our marketplace by having his coursework adjudicated. He did so, and discovered that he had to take just one additional course and he qualified to get his North American university degree in his field, **and** a professional designation. He did so, and was placed within a month.*

STEP 3i: Create the Education section

Add the Education section to your résumé template as shown here, and repeat if you have more than one degree or diploma.

Education

School, City, State/Province
Degree/Diploma/Designation   Year of Graduation.

Save the file!

COMPUTER SKILLS: I **did** say that Education was the last **Must Have**… but things have changed! Not too long ago the inclusion of your computer skills was not essential, and some people left it off entirely. With each passing year it increases in its value to show your technical savvy. I highly recommend you include this section for the following reasons:

- Junior applicants will find that due to their broad and sound computing skills, this is a section they can fill out thoroughly and have confidence in.

- Many companies will either use common software packages such as MS Office, or parts of it such as Word, Powerpoint, and Excel. Their ubiquity in the professional environment means that some applicants with inferior skills can be left behind. If you have sound background in these areas, reporting this on your résumé can help separate you from the pack.

- Some companies use their own licensed or designed proprietary software. If you can prove that you have a strong foundation in overall software skill, they will be more receptive to the idea that you can pick up quickly their package.

Many mid to senior level professionals often omit this section. While other skills rise in importance as an executive moves up the corporate ladder, a full complement of computer skills is seen as less relevant. I have had clients recently, however, looking for a Vice-President with a specific software skill, and well-qualified candidates without that one piece were passed by. Computer aptitude with systems, hard, and software experience clearly laid out is important for professionals at **every** level.

From a strength-of-format perspective, we've covered the main sections of a powerful résumé: Contact Information, Core Competencies, Experience/Accomplishments, and Education, and newcomer Computer Skills.

'Good to Have' Sections

While not explicitly mandatory, these sections can do a great deal to show a prospective employer that you have and continue to grow in the areas pertinent to your role. If any apply to your background or development, you should certainly include them.

PROFESSIONAL DEVELOPMENT: Companies love to know that someone looking for a role in their organization is committed to updating their skills over time and continuing to broaden their education. Examples of coursework, workshops and presentations attended, and so on that further your professional competency are best listed here.

PUBLICATIONS/PRESENTATIONS/PATENTS: Another non-vital section that many recruiters do like to see involves an applicant's contribution to their field. If you have published in your field, you should list that here. If you have given presentations to peers or professional groups, companies will want to know. Some professions encourage original ideas and patenting of innovative systems. If you have done so, include them! If you have none of these, leave it off your résumé entirely, and whichever of the three you don't have, delete it. So if, for example, you are a teacher and presented several lectures to your school staff or board members on 'Time Management for Teachers' and 'Keeping up with Student Computing Knowledge', entitle the section 'Presentations' and list this work. Employers love initiative, and when someone contributes to the body of knowledge of their profession, it shows a kind of commitment to the field that makes you shine.

AFFILIATIONS, MEMBERSHIPS, CERTIFICATION, LICENSES, ASSOCIATIONS, TRADE ORGANIZATIONS, MENTORSHIP, and VOLUNTEERISM: Participation in a group that has a direct connection to, or is a complement to your profession can be a great addition to your successful résumé.

An applicant may participate in a local, state or province-wide, or national organization that supports their industry. This is a career-based affiliation: If you are a CGA, or Certified General Accountant, that shows qualification. If further to that you sit on the local CGA board and chair meetings, you are seen as truly immersed in your field, and will have current and sometimes advance knowledge of new practices in your area. There are also civic affiliations, such as not-for-profit, community, and social groups. Career-based group connections are important to include on your résumé; civic-based are your choice.

Junior professionals want to fill up their résumé with the most **relevant** information, and more seasoned professionals need to pick and choose which to include. Career groups—good, civic groups—your choice. Again, delete from the title of this section those that don't apply to you and omit completely if it is not relevant.

LANGUAGES: Multilingualism can be a great advantage for an organization as they communicate with their international clients and counterparts. In Canada, fluency in French is a major boon, and Spanish is a great help for American businesses.

Do **not** list that you are fluent in English (yes, I've seen this…), as it will of course be assumed. Drawing attention to it will lead a recruiter to focus on possible communication issues when English is not your native language.

'Doesn't Matter' Sections

OBJECTIVE: The Objective, very commonly used and more commonly derided by recruiters has been in use for decades to clearly lay out what the applicant is looking for. It is most often placed directly under the Contact Information section and typically runs something like this:

<u>Objective:</u>

Top sales professional looking for a challenging position in a top organization where I can use my strong experience to contribute on a high level.

Blah, blah, blah…it's a bland sentence that says absolutely nothing about the person's real abilities or focus. Most often the more useful section, Core Competencies, already discussed, replaces the Objective.

A small number top companies surveyed did mention that having the Objective helped them keep straight which position that applicant had applied for. If it's not in the header of the email, or spelled out in the cover letter, a very simple Objective can be used:

Objective: To become a Sales Representative in the Diabetes Division of Bayer Inc.

It has also been argued that if you put your sought-after job title in an Objective, then it helps search engines find your résumé for that job, acting as a keyword. Keep in mind, however, that the honest use of keywords is not to trick a program into finding you. If you have the right experience and express it throughout the résumé you need not spell it out in an Objective. The only exception is when you are looking for a promotion to that new title and it's not to be found anywhere on the résumé.

Simple. Clear. Direct. The Objective can be a clerical tool to help a recruiter and keep your information organized. By and large, though, it takes up valuable space, and is rarely used by savvy, experienced candidates. Moreover, the specificity you use here can come back to haunt you. If, for example, you submit yourself to a company as a Sr. Marketing Manager, and include it in your objective…then a month later revise that to read Jr. Marketing Representative as you apply for a different role, it will be awkward for the recruiter to classify you.

This section is unnecessary; especially if you have the role you're applying to in the cover letter and subject line of your email submission.

HOBBIES, PERSONAL INTERESTS: Inclusion of your personal hobbies and interests may seem an innocuous addition. Applicants often feel either strongly about an avocation and wish to include it, or feel they can amuse or impress a recruiter with aspects of their private life. You may, however, inadvertently disclose information that could cause a recruiter to prejudge you. You are a volunteer with your political party; they may not vote the same way. You are a participant in a controversial group; it could work against you. Heck, even a sport you play *could* affect a recruiter's attitude towards you. They don't want to be influenced that way, so consider it very carefully if you choose to provide it. The only exception arises when a hobby or interest is directly related to something relevant to their company, issues, values, or the job description and can only be seen as a positive reflection.

> ## RÉSUMÉ SUCCESS 600 SURVEY HIGHLIGHT
>
> 33% of recruiters surveyed at top companies felt that it would be interesting to know about candidate Hobbies or Interests, but 53% said that it doesn't matter. Surprisingly, 11% replied that this section should absolutely *not* be included.

'Do Not Include' Sections:

PERSONAL INFORMATION: Date of birth, marital status, number of children, health, ethnicity, religion, and the full gamut of personal and private information do **not** have a place on a professional résumé! Laws in North America protect applicants from any form of discrimination and inclusion of such information is no longer appropriate. Volunteering this information is not correct protocol, and will hurt your chances as a recruiter will assume you are unfamiliar with most basic of submission principles. While this information is standard on résumés in many countries, you should consult with a North American résumé expert to have your information converted to a more palatable format.

ENDORSEMENTS: These are reference snippets or sales copy written by someone about your capability as a professional. **'Jennifer is the best seller in her territory! She's bright, always pushes herself, and sets the bar for others every month.' Jack Canlin—Sales Manager. Prada Sales** is an example. This section is a recent entry to résumé content and is not welcomed by most recruiters. New does **not** necessarily equal better, and it smacks of schmaltzy unprofessionalism.

The only exception here **may be** a junior professional who hasn't enough experience to fill 2 quality pages. Recruiters will take these in the right spirit in this case and it could help.

PHOTOGRAPHS: No. Just as with personal information, photographs are not to be included unless it's standard in your profession. Actors and models fit into this group.

A résumé is not supposed to be a profile including hobbies and interests like those you find on an Internet dating site…enjoying long walks on the beach and collecting action figures is not likely to interest a recruiter!
David Jerrett—Recruiter

SALARY INFORMATION: Never include your salary history or requirements on your résumé. You can easily be booted from the pile if your expectations are too lofty for their budget, and a low figure might mean that you're not worth the title. Never.

REASONS FOR LEAVING: Many people want to explain why they left a company, or feel they must. Lay-offs, restructuring, acquisitions, mergers, relocation, all are honest reasons for a person leaving an organization and are not often due to incompetence. For this reason they want to make it clear to a prospective employer that they aren't damaged goods! This is completely understandable…and unnecessary. Remember that recruiters are good at what they do, and they have their finger on the pulse of the employment industry; they know that your leaving a company doesn't mean you quit or were fired in a bad situation. Believe it or not they often **don't even want you** to include your reasons for leaving! They will always give you the benefit of the doubt and ask you in interview or by phone. If there is an instance that you feel needs to be explained you can do so in your cover letter, but not on your résumé.

Having said this, some applicants have been through numerous tragic circumstances requiring them to move several times in a short amount of time. If you are a contractor, you can list each role that was a contract position. If you were a full time employee and restructuring, downsizing, relocation of your division out of city or country or whatever required your company departure, you can list them on your résumé. In brackets beside your position you can list the reasons for the early move. Again, this is **only** in the case where numerous situations in which you were faultless caused you to leave when normally you would have remained and happily contributed.

Never state that you left a company 'for a better opportunity' elsewhere! Why on earth would a company want to hire a new employee who so readily admits they can be wooed to move to a competitor? I received such a résumé just two weeks ago…sigh.

RÉSUMÉ SUCCESS 600 SURVEY HIGHLIGHT

71% of recruiters responded that they DON'T want to see the reason for leaving, and that they will ask later. A further 7% said they would like questionable departures explained in the cover letter.

REFERENCES: Don't include them, or any mention of them.

Shocked??? It's true, there was a time when the last line of a résumé would always read: **'References available upon request'.**

Well now such a line is superfluous, as it will be assumed that every single applicant has their references in order. It saves you several lines of valuable space and is useless for a recruiter, so leave it off.

STEP 3j: Create final résumé sections

Update your Master Résumé Template with the 'Good to Have' and 'Doesn't Matter' sections you want to include. See the example on page 114–115, and save the template.

Save it!

You now have in your possession a Reverse Chronological Master Résumé Template containing all the key formatting ingredients to create a world-class résumé. Your fonts, sizing, format type, spacing, organization, sections are all in line with the top 5% of résumés submitted to top companies and recruitment agencies. Do not cut corners or ignore any of the advice in this chapter, as the **Résumé Success 600** research, with its millions of résumés and hundreds of years experience behind it, consistently reinforces that it works!

NAME
Street address, City, State/Province, zip/postal code
Phone: xxx-xxx-xxxx
Email

<u>Core Competencies</u>

Key strength
Key strength
Key strength
Key strength
Key strength
Key strength

<u>Professional Experience</u>

Job title, COMPANY, Location   mo/yr–mo/yr
Industry, product, size, revenues, scope, sector, placement

Responsibilities:
- Responsibility
- Responsibility
- Responsibility
- Responsibility
- Responsibility
- Responsibility
- Responsibility

Accomplishments:
- ○ Saved money/made money/process/awards/recognition
- ○ Saved money/made money/process/awards/recognition
- ○ Saved money/made money/process/awards/recognition

Job title, COMPANY, Location   mo/yr–mo/yr
Industry, product, size, revenues, scope, sector, placement

Responsibilities:
- Responsibility
- Responsibility
- Responsibility
- Responsibility
- Responsibility
- Responsibility
- Responsibility

Accomplishments:
- ○ Saved money/made money/process/awards/recognition
- ○ Saved money/made money/process/awards/recognition
- ○ Saved money/made money/process/awards/recognition

Job title, Company, Location   mo/yr–mo/yr
Industry, product, size, revenues, scope, sector, placement

Responsibilities:
• Responsibility
• Responsibility
• Responsibility
• Responsibility
• Responsibility
• Responsibility
• Responsibility

Accomplishments:
○ Saved money/made money/process/awards/recognition
○ Saved money/made money/process/awards/recognition
○ Saved money/made money/process/awards/recognition

Education

School, City, State/Province
Degree/diploma/designation/certification   Year of Graduation

School, City, State/Province
Degree/diploma/designation/certification   Year of Graduation

Computer Skills

Expert level proficiency in PROGRAM
Advanced proficiency in PROGRAM, PROGRAM, PROGRAM, and PROGRAM
Familiarity with PROGRAM

Memberships/Licenses

MEMBERSHIP
LICENSE

Languages

Fluent in written and spoken LANGUAGE, and conversational LANGUAGE

Hybrid Résumé Sections

For some there will be the need to steer clear, for the time being, of the Reverse Chronological format and settle for a Hybrid type. As mentioned earlier, this brings together several of the strengths of the Reverse Chronological format and several necessities of the Functional type of résumé. Let's make one thing clear, unless you are an executive, the Hybrid format is a compromise. If you cannot effectively create a RC formatted résumé do to lack of experience or otherwise, the Hybrid will get the job done. It is not the ideal, but better this than the full Functional, which specializes in cover-ups!

A correctly-built Hybrid résumé can reflect what experiences you do have with high effectiveness, while focusing primarily on the skills you possess to benefit your next employer in the role you are applying for.

Your goal should be to make the résumé as close as **possible** to the RC format with the understanding that as soon as your career experience allows you to, you switch to the widely embraced RC for good. You will create and save your template as a Hybrid for now, but when you can, switch to RC and save that as your new template to use for all future Master Résumés. So let's go through a strong Hybrid format, and where possible refer to slightly altered versions of RC sections rather than break from them and start from scratch.

CONTACT INFORMATION: Identical to the Reverse Chronological format, so read that section again and save your Résumé Template.

CORE COMPETENCIES: This section is identical to that of the RC format. However, in some cases you will not have a long enough list of quality professional experiences to distill down into this section to make it potent enough. To fix this, reduce the number of bullets to 4 or 6. If you can create more that are robust and compelling, include them!

RELEVANT SKILLS: In the RC résumé this next section would be to lay out your Professional Experience in its strongest form. Since your experience is **not** the thing to emphasize in this case, we take your Relevant Skill set and display it prominently as your key selling feature. Here's how to do it:

Think about the skills you have that are directly in line with the position you are considering. You may get some idea from the job description. Choose perhaps four or five areas. If you don't feel you can flesh out a heading with at least a few examples, then don't include it. Set it up on your template like this:

Relevant Skills:

Skill set #1—IE. Leadership
Example 1
2
3
4

Skill Set #2
Example 1
2
3
4

Skill Set #3
Example 1
2
3
4

Skill Set #4
Example 1
2
3
4

PROFESSIONAL EXPERIENCE: Next, use the Professional Experience section as with the RC formatted résumé. Be sure to include the company information and be honest with dates. Consolidate your responsibilities into fewer bullets; remember, we want the Skill Set to be prominent, and 15 bullets for Responsibilities will draw unwanted focus.

EDUCATION: Lay out just as with the Reverse Chronological format.

ALL OTHER SECTIONS: Follow the same rules as for the RC format.

That's it! Again, the emphasis in the most effective Hybrid résumé is to combine the strength of an RC format with the Skill Set focus of the Functional format.

Chapter 4 Summary

Master Key #3: FORMAT

- FORMAT: Avoid templates in general as they only provide one aspect of the truly successful résumé.
- FORMAT STYLES:
  - Use the Reverse Chronological format in almost every case
  - Use the Hybrid format if you have a significant challenge in making a RC formatted résumé
  - Use the CV format if for medical, academic, and scientific fields
- SOFTWARE: Save and send your résumé as a doc file; be sure to read the instructions on the site where you submit your résumé, as they will likely offer you clear direction.
- PAPER: Use plain paper in white or off-white color, 20–25 pound standard or with watermark, and never print on both sides of the page.
- FONTS:
  - Choose one font and stick with it
  - Don't mix fonts or overuse uppercase
  - Use bold, italics, and underlines sparingly and be consistent
  - Keep regular text between 10–12 pt, and font size hierarchy intact as you resize
- BULLETS: Essential, but do not mix bullet families.

- FLUSHED: The ragged right alignment works best so use that and nothing else. Use flush left margins aligning with the left edge for your résumé.

- MARGINS: Start with the default word processor settings. Then adjust when your résumé is complete for fit.

- WHITE SPACE: Very effective at providing balance and flow, positively affecting the readability of your résumé. Don't let your résumé be a chunk of crowded text.

- LINE SPACING: Double check your spacing to make sure that spaces between sections, subsections, and content are consistent throughout.

- TABS: Use tabs to group points, but don't overdo it.

- PAGE COUNT: If you can distill your qualifications down to two well balanced, non-cluttered, concise pages, then okay, do it. If three are required due to the amount of your relevant experience and ability, then be just as zealous in your editing.

REVERSE CHRONOLOGICAL FORMAT

- NAME: Make your name the most prominent thing on your résumé. Use the name you would like recruiters to refer to you as, and if you have a challenging name to pronounce and have a suitable nickname, use that. If you have a relevant designation, put it beside your name.

- ADDRESS: Enter your full mailing address in one or better yet two lines.

- PHONE NUMBER: Offer the best phone numbers to reach you at. Make sure that whatever number or numbers you leave are answered professionally, either voicemail or person and let the recruiter know when you will call back.

- CORE COMPETENCIES: Distilled listing of your career, quantitatively, with both hard and soft skills.

- PROFESSIONAL EXPERIENCE: Includes prior position title, company, location, dates employed, company synopsis, responsibilities, and accomplishments. It represents the bulk in size and importance on your résumé.

- MUST INCLUDE SECTIONS: Contact Information, Core Competencies, Experience, Accomplishments, Education, and Computer Skills.

- GOOD TO INCLUDE SECTIONS: Professional Development, Publications, Presentations, Patents, Affiliations, Memberships, Certification, Licenses, Associations, Trade Organizations, Mentorship, Volunteerism, and Languages.

- DOESN'T MATTER SECTIONS: Objective, Personal Interests and Hobbies.

- DO NOT INCLUDE: Personal Information, Photos, Endorsements, References, Salary Information, Reason for Leaving.

- HYBRID FORMAT: As above for Reverse Chronological format except two sections:

- RELEVANT SKILLS: Listing of preferred skill sets for applicant's profession, and quantitative examples provided.

- PROFESSIONAL EXPERIENCE: Offers a more consolidated set of experiences offset by robust skills section.

Chapter STEPS

STEP 3a: Set up your Master Résumé Template file

STEP 3b: Create the Contact Information section

STEP 3c: Create the Core Competencies section

STEP 3d: Create the Professional Experience section

STEP 3e: Create the Company Synopsis section

STEP 3f: Create the Responsibilities section

STEP 3g: Create the Accomplishments section

STEP 3h: Duplicate sections throughout résumé template

STEP 3i: Create the Education section

STEP 3j: Create final résumé sections

Slogans, jargon, quotations don't add to a résumé, but subtract. A good résumé tells me how much relative experience a person has, where they obtained it, what their specific role was, their accomplishments were, and why they're right for the role applied for. What-where-when-how-why.

Paul Farkas
—Sr. Recruiter,
David Aplin Recruiting

chapter 5

Master Key #4: CONTENT

The Content Master Key represents the words you choose and how you express yourself on your résumé. The phraseology, grammar, syntax, order, register, spelling, abbreviations, and other communicative means used make a great difference to how a recruiter ranks you versus other applicants. You use Content to build on a sturdy framework to create your masterpiece.

Content is that which makes your employment history come to life and sparkle; it evokes images of capability and competence in a recruiter's mind. Content is much more than eye candy, it represents the personality of your résumé. A brilliant career can be left dull and lifeless without sharp, powerfully presented Content. Done correctly, even a mediocre set of experiences can glow with tantalizing professionalism, attractive to recruiters in top companies and agencies alike.

This chapter covers the English essentials required for the most powerful résumé. The specific words you use will depend upon your unique situation. Chapters 6 and 8 will further expand on Content as we select those phrases most appropriate and potent for your own expression.

The Best Basics

In the English language there are certain conventions considered proper in communication. As an English teacher I used to cringe at the ongoing move away from traditional English with its elegant prose, to the byte-sized communication of text messaging and email today. Over time, however, I have resigned myself to the fact that this instant message-speak is nothing more than the most recent incarnation of a fast-evolving language.

The English of today outside the classroom is less about correctness and more about communication. If your audience is moved appropriately, has fully grasped your message in content and feeling and you are consistent, your English communication has done its job.

For general rules of the English language, Strunk and White's seminal book, *The Elements of Style*, has been for over 90 years **the** most influential touchstone against which truly correct writing should be measured.

However, a résumé is **not** an essay, and not related to any traditional form of English prose. Only the cover letter retains the near-proper grammatical form, as we will cover in Chapter 7. The impact of English in a résumé comes from the use of verbs and quantitative facts. Most other aspects are reduced or omitted entirely. It has become its **own** form of English expression, and as such has evolved some interesting grammatical conventions. Many of these adhere to the traditional rules, and others diverge for the sake of brevity and focus. The sections below reflect this new grammatical reality. Embrace them and your résumé will become tight, focused, and powerful. Ignore them at your professional peril.

SPELLING: Yes, yes, I know. You want to skip to the next section because of course **you** would **never** have a spelling mistake in **your** résumé, right? Yes, you would. I've seen it. From $20,000 a year call centre staff to $250,000 Vice-Presidents, I've seen innumerable errors that stretch from the comical to the painfully awkward.

Let's get one thing clear because this is the case for every single résumé regardless of experience or level:

There is *no* excuse for poor spelling.

None.

If, in our 5-second initial scan we discover a spelling error, it's likely that you will go straight into the garbage. If you're lucky a recruiter will forgive one oversight if you are otherwise an outstanding fit, but why on earth would you set yourself up for such quick potential failure?

Mistakes in spelling can manifest themselves in a number of ways: Of course the most obvious is an outright typo, like spelling exercise 'excercise'. The word processing software of today can easily catch such errors. My MS Word program has just underlined the faulty 'excercise' with a wiggly red line to let me know it needs fixing, and indeed it can be set to correct such faults automatically. This, however, can lead to a kind of spelling complacency that I think is the most direct reason for the tremendous number of spelling problems in résumés today.

We are becoming accustomed to accepting the computer as our default spelling instructor. If I write a sentence or three and no red lines indicate an error, or in a spell check when I'm done nothing is flagged as a mistake, I assume that it's perfect! The challenge is that while it **will** catch outright misspellings in most cases, it will **not** catch improper **use** of words. If you mean to write 'Chaired Senior's Committee' and you leave off the 'C', you've just told the recruiter you 'Haired' the committee…and while they **may** need hair, the recruiter won't be laughing. Your software program will **not** catch improper use of words. The majority of these mistakes occur when a correctly spelled but improperly used work is inserted. You use **there** instead of **their,** you accidentally leave off a letter and **the** becomes **he,** you do an edit and leave errant words in the text…we recruiters see it far too often.

We hate it.

Here's what you need to do in order to avoid this issue:

1. Use the spellchecker on your software as a **start**.

2. Read the document out loud from start to finish several times. You will catch a number of errors this way. You may also find there are some words you are not sure you have used correctly or not, so you can check with a dictionary.

> *I find it incredible that highly educated people who are relied upon in business to give accurate, critical, and detailed reports so often misspell in their own résumé submission! It destroys all credibility.*
>
> Tom Rainey—
> Executive Recruiter,
> Novus Reputo Recruiting

3. **Always** check the spelling of people and company names on your résumé.

4. Give the résumé to a trusted 3rd party. They best be a native English speaker to understand the full nuances of the language, and ideally someone with a professional or educational background in English.

Do them *all*. You may feel as though it's a bit embarrassing giving your résumé to another for a proofread, but sometimes that fresh set of eyes can save you from making a dangerous résumé faux pas. I read over the text of this book four times before sending it to an editor and **every** time through it I caught errors…and then he caught more. When it came back to me, I found **more**.

RÉSUMÉ SUCCESS 600 SURVEY HIGHLIGHT

We asked the top agency and corporate recruiters to give insight into the importance of spelling and how it affects a résumé. Here are some telling points:

- When asked, 'What is a reflection of a GREAT résumé?' several respondents from very different industries wrote the identical answer: *perfect spelling*

- **When asked about their Top 3 Résumé Pet Peeves, *'Spelling' came up more than any other error or omission***

- When polled about how many mistakes they would allow before they threw out the résumé regardless of how good the experience was, 77% of recruiters surveyed said they would let one spelling error pass if the applicant was otherwise a great fit, but a second mistake and they're gone! This includes improper use of words and grammatical errors.

PERSONAL PRONOUNS: The résumé and all its content is a reflection of **you**, remember. It is a necessarily biased document, and since it's authorship and focus is assumed, typical pronouns can be omitted. First person singular 'I', or plural 'we', second person singular or plural 'you', and third person singular 'he/she' and plural 'they' should be left off your résumé.

While you're at it, dump the objective 'we/us', the reflexive 'myself/ ourselves', and the possessive 'my/our/mine/ours'. You will see shortly how we diminish and omit such conventions in order to draw out the impact of action verbs and quantitative, high-impact facts.

Also, don't ever refer to yourself in the 3rd person on your résumé, or in interview. Yes, it does happen. 'David accomplished 18 of 20 performance objectives' on my résumé is unnecessary, distracts a reader from the impact of my bullet points…and recruiters know I wrote it…so that's just weird.

TENSE: Use of consistent and correct verb tense is an easy and often ignored ingredient in a successful résumé. When you outline your Responsibilities and Accomplishments, we recruiters often find inconsistencies, even within one role. Consider the list, '**ran** a $490,000 branch', '**finds** opportunities for cost savings', and '**Had discovered** daily discrepancies in sales targets'. As separate responsibility items for the same position, they mix tense and show an inconsistency that a recruiter will notice. While it's both common and painful for a recruiter to read, it's not difficult to overcome.

If you are listing a company at which you are currently still employed, use the present tense in your description, minus the personal pronoun 'I'. You would write, '**Sell** widgets in 18 different national regions'. For all other companies at which you no longer work, your verb tenses will be in past form, like, '**Sold** widgets in 18 different national regions'.

CAPITALIZATION: Position titles are usually capitalized in résumés. It adds a feeling of importance and emphasis to them. A general rule on the résumé is that capital letters draw attention to something, attributing to it greater respect. **Senior Programmer**, then, feels superior to a **senior programmer**, and acceptable to capitalize. Similarly, it's common practice on to emphasize departments in capital form. You didn't work in the **marketing department**, you worked in the **Marketing Department**. As you see, it brings out the polish and esteem of the role and area.

Don't go too far, though, by emphasizing through capitalization too much in one section:

OVERDOING IT: *Assisted the Marketing, Sales, and IT Departments and presented to Steering Committee including the Vice-President, Managers, and Supply Chain Specialists*

Take some time to work your bullets for clout and don't be too liberal with your use of capitals.

INSIDER SECRET

Many résumé creators will stick to proper English form, which actually *detracts* from the power your job titles, departments, and the like show to a reader. Recruiters aren't English specialists, they're résumé specialists. Emphasize the right areas and help them help you.

COLONS: Even as we destroy some long-standing rules of grammar for use in your résumé, some conventions remain. There are numerous uses for colons, but let's cover the few that will be relevant to your ultimate résumé:

The general rule holds that the colon is used to separate two clauses. The latter amplifies or interprets the earlier. While doing this, you cannot separate a verb from its complement or a preposition from its object.

INCORRECT: *Accounting Department grew: by hiring staff, increasing responsibilities, and merging divisions*

The above is wrong because it takes the verb **grew** away from its complementary list of hiring staff, increasing responsibilities, and merging divisions. A more correct example follows.

CORRECT: *Grew the Accounting Department in three ways: hired staff, increased responsibilities, and merged divisions*

You see the first clause can stand on it's own, and the second clause helps explain it.

Now let's look at the next issue, where a colon cannot separate a preposition from its object.

INCORRECT: *Acted upon key recommendations from: Municipal, State, and Federal departments*

CORRECT: *Acted upon key recommendations from several departments: Municipal, State, and Federal*

Having said this, remember very few recruiters are English majors, and should you make mistakes in your use of colons, or the semicolons that follow, you may sneak through without issue. But now that you know how to use them correctly, do it!

SEMICOLONS: The semicolon is used in several ways, but in its essence it joins two completely independent clauses that relate to each other. Each clause could stand on its own as a sentence, but a period is too strong, and a comma is too soft. Here a semicolon can be used.

I have seen use of the semicolon abused more even than the colon. Steer clear of using it in your résumé except in the following case: When you are creating a list in which there is repetition of some aspect, the semicolon acts as a buffer.

EXAMPLE: *Submitted accounting reports to governmental agencies representing full disclosure of inside practices; full accountability by management; and full acceptance of all implications*

Another example shows that when you have a series of three or more items that would normally be separated by commas that already have them.

EXAMPLE: *Invited to Peak Performer Dinner for outstanding sales performance January, February, March; May, June, July; and October, November, and December of 2009*

ARTICLES: Articles such as 'a', 'an', 'the', so very common in a regular sentence, are used only sparingly in a résumé. Again, the English in a résumé is used to bring to the surface the important facts about yourself that will showcase your abilities and help a recruiter evaluate your fit for the role. Articles, then, are so much background noise, and we delete most of them so long as their absence doesn't destroy the message.

INCORRECT: *Implemented an ongoing improvement plan, which resulted in a net timesaving of 130% in a high-pressure environment*

CORRECT: *Implemented ongoing improvement plan resulting in net timesaving of 130% in high-pressure environment*

Neat and clean, and the remaining parts of the point are sharp and meaningful. You don't need to remove **every** article, however. If the sentence you begin with has three or more articles, you may want to leave one in. In the above example the final 'a' could remain. You want it to be as lean as possible while retaining a readable message.

PREPOSITIONS: Connective words introducing prepositional phrases such as **at, with, through, between, from, by, to,** and **in** are called prepositions. Just as with articles, prepositions can make your otherwise powerful attributes feel more wordy than necessary. You may find opportunities within a résumé phrase, especially if there are multiple prepositions together, to pare down and make the group more lean.

WORDY: *Asserted authority through meetings in teams, and at the factory*

BETTER: *Asserted authority through team and factory meetings*

ADJECTIVES: Restrain yourself from the use of excessive adjectives or describing words in the creation of your résumé. You want to impress, but adjectives alone will make you come off as a blowhard, and are often unspecific.

INCORRECT: *Offered world-class service to powerful client groups resulting in successful sales, massive growth, and incredible bottom-line profits.*

This is a very common mistake, and we recruiters hate it. 'World-class', 'powerful', 'successful', 'massive', 'incredible'…all great adjectives, but they don't **say** anything! They are general and largely subjective descriptors, and recruiters will see right through it and consider you a braggart. You **do** want to toot your own horn, but if you do, back it up with facts!

> **CORRECT:** *Serviced clients groups from 15 of the highest grossing companies in North America, resulting in an increase in sales of 124%, growth of 13 stores, and net profit increase of $3.5M*

In this example we've taken out the bluster of adjectives and replaced them with such powerful quantitative facts that a recruiter cannot help but be impressed.

ABBREVIATIONS: Abbreviations are used to shorten a word or phrase to save space, and assumes that the reader will understand the abbreviated form. Instead of writing out 'department', you could abbreviate to 'dept.'. One might think that they should be used liberally in a résumé because all our instruction has pushed a tight, lean, mean format. While this is generally true, there are a few important reservations to go over.

> *It's like Joe Friday used to say, "I want the facts. Just the facts."*
> John Perry—
> Vice-President,
> David Aplin
> Recruiting.

We went over the use of keywords in your résumé so that scanning software, bots, and spidering will be able to find your relevance to a potential position more easily. If you have certain short forms common in society, then you might find good cause to include them. For example, **Master of Arts Degree** can be shortened to **M.A.** or even **MA** to fit beside your name in the Contact Information section. I would still recommend spelling it out in its entirety in your Education section, though, as the words have clout and you don't know how the recruiter will search for the degree.

On the other hand, what if you commonly use an abbreviation in your line of work that might not be known by the general public. If you work in product marketing, you know that a unique alphanumeric number that is associated with a product in a store is called a **'stock-keeping unit'**. This is most often reduced to the abbreviated form, **'sku'**. When including this in your résumé, you must be **certain** that a recruiter, who may have little understanding of your area of specialization, will understand the abbreviated form, and just as important, use it as a keyword when they search Internet and database résumés to find someone with your qualifications.

Imagine you have a lengthy history in the area of **Accounts Payable**, commonly called **A/P**. You populate your résumé with the abbreviation since it's common in your area. A recruiter, who has just moved from recruiting for another department and is new to accounting initiates a search on her computer, and uses the keywords **Accounts Payable**, not familiar with the abbreviation. Your résumé comes back as a poor match, not because you weren't a great fit, but because you used the abbreviation exclusively!

Use, then, abbreviations when they are universally known and used, or mix them with long form for coverage. Anything that can be considered lingo, and so not known to people unfamiliar to your field should be avoided.

While the Internet has been called the **Web**, and **Net**, the most common and a present accepted term is still the **Internet**…so use that.

SENTENCES: As you read over this chapter you may be feeling that on a résumé we put the traditional idea of a sentence in the back seat…worse, in the **trunk** and rely upon punchy facts. This is absolutely true. As mentioned, a powerful résumé leaves behind personal pronouns, many of the sentence articles we've come to use so commonly, and other commonly used conventions in order to shout out byte sized bullets that highlight your brilliance.

There is no need for sentences in a great résumé.

VERBS: There are two main verb types to pay attention to when crafting your best résumé; we give the boot to one type and lovingly embrace and polish the other.

Auxiliary verbs, also called helping verbs, such as **be**, **keep** or **keeps**, **have**, **has**, **am**, **is**, **are**, **was**, **were**, **been**, **should**, **can**, **could**, **shall**, **must**, **might**, **may**, **does**, **did**, **do**, and the like. Just as we removed the majority of articles, so too, we remove most if not all auxiliary verbs. They make our comments longer and they take focus away from your real areas of emphasis.

INCORRECT: *The Procurement Department had developed a new strategy*

CORRECT: *The Procurement Department developed a new strategy*

It's just as clear, but more succinct.

The **real** power in verb use comes from **ACTION verbs**. An outstanding résumé is rife with powerful verbs that lead off a bullet point detailing your experience. Compare the following responsibility sets; the first reflects the traditionally crafted tedium, and the second uses verbs effectively.

OLD: *Took out older reporting policies to help processes improve in the areas of audit and due diligence*

NEW: ***Abolished*** *inefficient reporting policies, improving audit and due diligence*

OLD: *Was responsible for approval of many aspects of product, such as packaging, pricing, and placement in stores.*

NEW: ***Approved*** *full range of product packaging, pricing, and placement of products to achieve*

OLD: *Brought into one facility all manufacturing in order to reduce shipping costs*

NEW: ***Consolidated*** *manufacturing to one plant, reducing shipping costs by 15%*

OLD: *Came up with a new way of processing new employees to move them more quickly from new hire to working the floor*

NEW: ***Pioneered*** *innovative training program, resulting in significant cuts in timelines from new hire to successful floor salesperson*

It's amazing how a slight rewording, beginning with a strong, image-evoking verb can really bring experiences, responsibilities, and accomplishments to life!

Every résumé preparation book I reviewed seemed to have a listing of action verbs. Some were quite short, and others exhaustively long. I vacillated as to whether or not, based on the research, they would be worthwhile to include. In case you haven't realized by now, this book is not at all about what has gone before, what is **common**, but rather what we know to be current, researched, and truthful in résumé design from the insider perspective to bring it to excellence.

So I decided against it.

Here's why: The most common use of action verb lists causes a job seeker to scan the list, find a compelling verb they think applies to their role, then construct a point around that powerful lead in. On the surface this seems reasonable, but it's inverting the proper order. You should decide **first** upon your most powerful quantitative point, as it is the key aspect of the bullet, **then** select the most appropriate, vivid action word to introduce that fact.

You don't scan a long list, find 'pioneer', for example, decide that was a great verb and you **had** started new things you want a recruiter to know about, then come up with an example of something you had pioneered.

Instead, you must decide on a key fact, such as your creation of a new filing system, come up with a quantitative fact about the extent to which that saved money/made money, or improved a process, and **then** consider the most potent verb to introduce the fact.

It then becomes 'Pioneered new filing system process, leading to 38% reduction in lost invoices'. Fantastic!

The 'pioneer' is an evocative verb and works well to draw the attention of a recruiter, but it in itself is not the key point. You could have used 'devised' or 'implemented', or 'created', or 'engineered', or even 'introduced' or 'initiated'...all these would have readily suited your purpose.

Sometimes it's the case that an applicant has decided on their point but can't think of how to lead into it with anything but a common, dull verb. Scanning a long list of action verbs is a tedious, unnecessary, and wasteful way to come to their best choice. Also, oftentimes they read the entire list and don't find a fit!

Here's the answer.

If, after you decide upon the key point to express in that bullet, you can't come up with an action verb remotely appropriate, use a thesaurus. MS Word makes this easy. If I wrote the word 'started', and I feel that's too bland and want to spice it up, I just select it, right click (control click on a Mac), and choose 'synonyms' from the drop down box for a list of similar words. In this case it came up with **create, found, begin, establish, set up, initiate, institute, launch, pioneer,** and **inaugurate**! Instant action word list! You may have to select the root of the word, being 'start' in this case, in order to access the full list of synonyms. There are also countless online thesauri to help as well.

If this doesn't work for you, simply find a list online. I recently checked and a search for 'action verb list' brought me 1.7 million hits. I visited a number of them and they all contained the identical type of examples you'd find in a typical verb list.

If you're really stuck, send me a note at **david@davidjgardner.com** and I'll help you.

The inclusion of powerful action words to represent your contributions while with past employers is very appealing for recruiters. Do **not** embellish, however. If you wrote, 'Implemented new program reducing Accounts Receivable by 24%', then you must have been in some way responsible for the implementation, even as a team member, advisor, or key member. If you just happed to be there when it took place, then you can't take credit for it!

COMMAS: Commas can be very useful in a document where brevity and succinctness are required.

Of course the comma is most often used to separate three or more items in a listed series, such as, 'Grew client lists, sales region, and presentation opportunities.'

They can replace 'and' as in 'Achieved recognized increase in scope, depth of client relationships.'

Commas can be used to increase the effectiveness of a single, powerful, bulleted point.

INCORRECT: *Pioneered new product rollout technique ahead of schedule that led to a 34% increase in point-of-sales profit*

CORRECT: *Pioneered new product rollout technique ahead of schedule, leading to a 34% increase in point-of-sale profits*

> *Before you can 'dress to impress' when going to an interview, your résumé must do that first. It's a personal reflection of who you are and what you stand for. Do it right!*
>
> Sumbo Ashabo— Recruitment Team Lead, Ceridian Canada

Read the above sentences aloud. The comma used in the latter example provides an additional perceptual break in the sentence, taking one longer factual byte and creating two smaller ones. Easier to absorb this way, the comma succeeds in increasing the punch of a single quality point.

HYPHENS: In general, the hyphen is used to join numbers or words together. If the joined words are verbs, they don't usually carry the hyphen.

> **EXAMPLE:** *Ran* **eighty-four** *concurrent sessions on system implementation.*

Note: as covered, you would simply list the Arabic numeral 84 in your résumé, but write it in full on a cover letter.

> **EXAMPLE: Carried on** *multiple client conversations at once*

The verb phrase from 'to carry on' above would not by hyphenated. However, if the terms are nouns or adjectives, they sometimes pick up the hyphen, and other times join together as one compound word.

> **EXAMPLE:** *Envisioned and created* **high-quality** *processes for refinement*
>
> **EXAMPLE:** *Responsible for* **overlooked** *import product costs*

They hyphen can be best used in a résumé to combine adjectives and increase the flow through your selected points. The above '**high-quality**' draws a higher focus than two separate words, so use them where possible.

DASHES: The dash has emerged as a common substitute for other marks of punctuation, such as the colon, semicolon, or even the comma. Not to be confused with the tiny hyphen, the smaller of the dashes is called the 'en' dash, which is twice a hyphen's size.

Its most common use on a résumé is to show the length of time an individual worked at one role, and separating phone digits.

Twice as long and more popular recently is the 'em' dash. Used for emphasis as it replaces other marks, the *em* dash can also improve white space and provides an even more visual break in information than the comma.

EXAMPLE: *Grew the Accounting Department in three ways— hired staff, increased responsibilities, and merged divisions (replaces the colon)*

EXAMPLE: *Aggressively reduced patient wait times through new triage protocols—saving an average 67 minutes per emergency shift (replaces a comma)*

hyphen -

en dash –

em dash —

There are other, more creative uses for the *em* dash, and it does seem to work for a recruiter. It is not unattractive, lessens clutter, and can be used to emphasize words or phrases more than standard punctuation can. I have seen it overused and misused, however, and its use comes with a caveat: if you lack sufficient comfort with the language to be able to experiment with the *em* dash to see if it works—avoid it.

ELLIPSES: Traditionally used to indicate that a part of a quotation has been omitted, the ellipsis, or three consecutive periods, has evolved to imply that there is more to be said than provided. It can provide a dramatic pause:

EXAMPLE: *A résumé too full of ellipses can go...unread.*

It can also leave a sense of something profound and unfinished:

EXAMPLE: *He told me if I sent my résumé he'd call me...*

In a résumé the most common appearance of the ellipsis appears when a candidate uses it to separate achievements or in a summary of skills:

EXAMPLE: *Overachieved targets... top seller... management recognized... professionally dressed... well-qualified.*

This is useless to a recruiter and poor form. Useful in many situations, the ellipsis is of little use on a résumé, so avoid using it.

ETC: **Etc**, or '**etcetera**' fully, has become ubiquitous in written English use. Its purpose is to suggest to the reader 'and so forth', or 'more of this sort of thing'. The problem on a résumé is that you need to be succinct but fully expressive of your talents. You cannot possibly expect a recruiter reading your résumé or cover letter to fill in the blanks and attribute additional skills, experiences, or education that you have left off due solely to use of the *etc*! Specificity dictates that you clearly detail every significant attribute necessary to get that interview, so the etc has no place on your résumé **or** in your cover letter.

NUMBERS: Numbers represent another area of your résumé where we must sidestep tradition and go for what works best with recruiters. There is little agreement in English circles which is more correct, spelling out each individual number as a word, or using the Arabic number itself. Most commonly one is instructed to list the numbers **one** through **nine** as words, and **10** and beyond in the Arabic form (inserting the numerals). Compound word numbers such as **ninety-four thousand** are traditionally spelled out.

Such lengthy numbers pose a problem for the word-thrifty résumé writer. Indeed, even on the cover letter one would be loathe to write out, 'I saved the company four hundred sixty-two *million, eight hundred thousand and twenty-two dollars.'*

Gasp.

On your cover letter, after the one to nine exceptions, use Arabic numerals. This allows you to tip your had to tradition and show you can use written numbers as expected, while saving space and demonstrating the impact of the Arabic numbers as well.

Never begin a sentence with an Arabic numeral.

On your résumé you can either follow the same model, or go even further and remove all spelling out of numbers. Remember, as a punchy self-advertising document, numbers speak loudly, shouting above words as recruiters scan for quantitative ways you excel versus your peers.

CONTRACTIONS: Contractions are used to combine and shorten two separate words with an apostrophe. **It is** becomes **it's**, and **does not** becomes **doesn't**. While the conservation of space where possible remains important, the use of contractions serves to reduce the level or formality of your document. You must evaluate your audience and determine if contractions are warranted; you might not want to show a level of familiarity or friendliness to a Résumé Gatekeeper who has never heard of you before and risk offending her.

There is no absolute right or wrong answer here, except to be consistent once you have chosen. It is always safest to err on the side of conservatism and shy away from contraction use.

PERIODS: A period is used to complete a sentence. We have already covered the idea that there are no sentences in a résumé, and so there is no need for sentence periods…period!

Even if your bullet point responsibilities or accomplishments somehow end up appearing as a sentence, avoid wrapping them up in a period.

In your cover letter, on the other hand, you will need periods to complete each sentence. If you use bullet points there, you should use periods to end any point that reads as a sentence.

> *Show me what you have accomplished and include numbers where possible. Phrases can be subjective (i.e., processed a large number of invoices) whereas numbers are more factual and powerful (i.e., processed 1,000 invoices per week).*
> Rakesh Kothary— Sr. Search Consultant, Mason Group Recruiting.

EXAMPLE: *Comprehensive reviews of proposal standards led to 42 new efficiency rules. (period used)*

EXAMPLE: *Success achieving 132% of sales quota (no period required)*

Other uses of the period:

EXAMPLE: *M.B.A. (Abbreviation)*

EXAMPLE: *Mr. John Bascombe (titles)*

It should be mentioned that while the use of two spaces after a period ending sentence has been in use for the majority of the existence of the obsolete typewriter, its importance and use has waned. It was necessary to allow for the appropriate amount of space to carry the eye between sentences in typewritten non-proportional mono-spaced typefaces. Technology now provides proportional fonts that give an *em* space between sentences, and makes the double space stand out as awkward. You can see that sentences in this book are separated by a single space.

Charts & Graphs

Nope.

By now you know that being different isn't always good in the world of recruiting talent. Don't assume that a graphical representation of your sales achievements over the past nine fiscal quarters is going to impress the Résumé Gatekeeper. If it even hints at being a flashy gimmick you may not make it past the 5-second screen.

The only exception exists if there is a standard graph or chart that is a key representation of your abilities that is both expected by a potential hiring manager and easy to grasp by the recruiter. Then you can consider using one…perhaps.

RÉSUMÉ SUCCESS 600 SURVEY HIGHLIGHT

84% of recruiters surveyed tell us that a chart or graph has no place on a résumé, period. The remaining 16% specified that *only* if it had absolute relevance would they consider it.

The above list is in fact, only partial, but contains the most often used and mistaken English content mistakes in résumés. Your proofreader will be able to catch any further minor misstep you make.

As you reel from the sheer volume of specific content-related information thrown at you in this chapter, let's conclude with a reminder mentioned several times so far. The guidelines outlined in this chapter are rules based on **what recruiters like to see in your résumé** and **not** what a professor of English would suggest!

Sometimes they overlap and sometimes they're at odds, but it's an important distinction! Many résumé specialists feel they are well qualified to create or fix your résumé because they excel at English. Not only might this **not** be an advantage, their focus on the traditional rules of grammar may **ruin** your success by bogging down your résumé with structure and content that doesn't appeal to a recruiter. The résumé is about a specific and unique form of English communication and all you need do is follow the instructions laid out here and don't worry about calls from the language police.

At its core, the Content of your résumé is all about effective communication.

You will use the Content rules and distinctions you learned here as we bring together the first four Keys and build your Master Résumé next chapter.

Chapter 5 Summary

Master Key #4: CONTENT

- **General**: The common rules of grammar do not apply uniformly in a résumé, and even the cover letter bends some traditional rules.

- **Spelling**: Correct spelling is a must. Don't trust a program or yourself to be the ideal proofreader for your résumé.

- **Personal Pronoun**: No personal pronouns. Don't refer to yourself in 3rd person.

- **Tense:** If you're still there, use present verb tense. All others will be past.

- **Capitalization**: In addition to traditional words to capitalize, do so also with position titles and departments. Don't overdo it.

- **Colon:** Use a colon to separate two clauses. Avoid them unless you're comfortable with their use. Minor colon errors can usually pass undetected.

- **Semicolon**: Don't worry too much about adding the semicolon to your résumé, but using the provided forms is correct usage.

- **Article:** Remove most articles from your points to streamline your message. You need not remove them all, so long as you are consistent.

- **Preposition**: Wherever possible, streamline phrases, removing excessive prepositions.

- **Adjective**: Wherever possible, replace a self-aggrandizing adjective with a more powerful fact.

- **Abbreviation**: Common abbreviations are fine, but be cautious. If you feel there's any chance a recruiter won't understand the abbreviation, then you could spell it out in full at first, and use the abbreviation later, or stick with the full word or phrase.

- **Sentence**: It's true; there need not be **any** sentences in an excellent résumé today. The fact-based, bytes of information you include are just what the recruiter needs and are **extremely** effective at getting your professional message across.

- **Verbs:** Avoid filler auxiliary verbs and apply powerful action verbs to bring your presentation to its highest level.

- **Commas**: Use the comma to join lists, replace otherwise-superfluous words such as 'and', and break a point into two more potent sub-facts. Other uses of the comma are inefficient since full sentences are not found on a strong résumé.

- **Dashes**: The *em* dash can be very effectively used in your résumé. If you choose to replace punctuation with the *em* dash do it consistently by section or on the entire résumé. Do not overuse it.

- **Ellipses**: You needn't have use of an ellipsis anywhere on your résumé.

- **ETC**: Never use etc on your résumé or cover letter.

- **Numbers**: Cover letter, spell out one through nine and above use Arabic numerals. Résumé, either do the same, or even better use Arabic numbers exclusively.

- **Contractions**: Best not to use them, but if you do, be consistent.

- **Periods**: While there are no sentence periods required on a résumé, they should be used, with one space afterwards, on a cover letter. Abbreviations and titles can use a period, but sometimes are omitted with little impact. Be consistent.

- **Charts and Graphs**: Unless your profession has a requirement that can best be shown in graph or chart for **and** you are positive it will be well received, it's best not to consider including one on your résumé.

The percentage of candidates that understand the true importance of a résumé is too low! This is their chance to shine above all others… 'toot' their own horn! I can't tell you how many people have claimed to have great 'attention to detail', but their résumé has spelling mistakes, is formatted horribly, or has different fonts and bullet types. If applicants don't put the work in to make sure their résumé is perfect, why would I think they would be successful in the role I'm recruiting for??

Shireen Dietrich
—Manager, PTC Accounting
and Finance Recruiting

chapter 6

Let's Build It!

Now it's magic time!

We've covered 4 of the **5 Master Keys to Résumé Success:** foundational **Knowledge,** accumulated **Experience,** effective **Format,** and rules of **Content.** The fifth and final Key, **Submission,** will come once we're ready to release your masterpiece into the world. We've reached a point at which we can combine all we've done so far into your Master Résumé; the source for every résumé you will build going forward!

STEP 4a: Create your Master Résumé document file

Open up your saved résumé template. As we make changes and develop it into your Master Résumé, you'll need to save the file under a different heading than you have now so that you can keep the template file unaltered for possible future use if you or anyone you know needs to build a résumé from scratch. Save your Master Résumé using a name that will be easily understood by a recruiter and makes their organizational life easier. **'resume.doc'** will be the name of countless files they import, so better to name yours clearly. Remember to use the **Save As** option, which will save this as a separate file and leave your template intact. If you choose 'Save' alone, it will overwrite your template file with this, which we don't want.

A file name such as **'davidjgardner_sales_resume.doc'** or similar is best, including name, field, and type of document. Some newer versions of MS Word allow you to save without the underscore '_', and include an actual space, which makes it all the more attractive. If it appears too long with your title, then reduce it to full name and 'résumé'. Ideally you want it to be personal to you, professional to them, and contain information that will help them file and find you easily.

If you choose to put the month or year in your résumé file title… make **sure** you update it before sending it anywhere.

As we go through the well-formatted résumé template you've got saved and populate it with your experience while adhering to the best rules of Content, I will demonstrate, creating a fictitious sales résumé with you.

STEP 4b: Populate the Contact Information with your own personal details

---

DAVID J. GARDNER MBA
1313 Mockingbird Lane, Toronto, ON, M4W 2H8
Cell: 416-389-4986
davidjgardner_sales@gmail.com

Save it!

STEP 4c: Populate the Professional Experience area with your own information

Skip the **Core Competencies** part for the moment (we need information from the next sections to complete it) and let's build your **Professional Experience** section. Highlight and fill in your position title, the company name, location, and the dates you worked there for each role. If you think you may have too many positions to list and you don't know where to stop, err on the side of listing too many for the time being, and we can edit them down later.

Look it over so far. It should start clean and end up clean, your font is clear, your information easy on the eyes. Your spacing and margins are retained and flow neatly and the dates should be aligned vertically in harmony.

DAVID J. GARDNER MBA
1313 Mockingbird Lane, Toronto, ON, M4W 2H8
Cell: 416-389-4986
davidjgardner_sales@gmail.com

Core Competencies

Key strength
Key strength
Key strength
Key strength
Key strength
Key strength

Professional Experience

Sales Manager, THE TURKEY PALACE, Toronto   June '06-Present

STEP 4d: Create a Company Synopsis from your Chapter 3 notes

Bring out your Experience notes from Chapter 3 and read over **Step 2a: Company Synopsis.** Let's take this information and create one powerful and abbreviated synopsis about what they represent as a business on the following line. Remember, the better **they** look, the better **you** look. Let me give you an example using my notes for The Turkey Palace:

Company Clout:

> **Company name**: The Turkey Palace
> **Industry:** Manufacturer/distributor
> **# of employees:** ?
> **# of facilities:** 29 Stores
> **Local/national/international:** International

Which cities, states, provinces, and countries: 15 largest
cities in North America
Place in industry vs competitors: 10th or more
Private/public/traded where: public, listed on New York
Stock Exchange
Years in business: 6
Interesting facts/firsts: The first manufacturer of 0% fat
ground turkey and popular 'John's' brand
Annual Revenues: ?
Annual Sales: ?
Average Growth: 58% since creation

You can see that there are some areas in which this company
impresses, and others that are merely ordinary. In fact, there are a few
areas I have no information at all. The advantage of creating an extensive list about the company is that it's then easy to find now a couple
of key points that set it apart from its competition. The Turkey Palace is
not even close to being number 1 in its industry, for example. It doesn't
have an especially high number of employees, or many facilities in
Canada and the US. However, it was the **first** of its kind, and with loca-
tions in both Canada and US it is legitimately international in scope.
Also, while only 29 stores, they **are** in the largest cities. Bringing this
together, here is a great **Company Synopsis.**

International manufacturer/distributor of poultry products with
stores in 15 major North American cities and average annual growth of
58% since inception, NYSE: TPPi

Just one phrase and yet it conveys a great amount of useful information for a recruiter. Let's have a closer look:

International is the largest scope a business can operate, larger
than local, province or statewide, or national. This means as a professional may have dealt with cross-border issues, trade agreements, cur-
rency exchange, reporting to a foreign head office, or other possible
issues.

Manufacturer/distributor is important. **You** may believe that everyone should know your company's field and focus, but you shouldn't

assume that. Helping a recruiter out by informing her of the industry you worked in will help, especially if it's the same, or at least a related industry to the one you're applying to!

Poultry products tells the recruiter a little about what it was the company sold.

Stores in 15 major N.A. cities relates to the high market penetration. Your company plays in a big pond.

Average annual growth of 58% since inception is an impressive statistic for the company. You needn't say they've only been in business for 6 years, that's not important. Sustained growth is sexy for hiring companies.

NYSE: TTPi If your company is publically traded, you can include the stock name and exchange here as well. If the organization wasn't trending positively when you worked there, you may want to leave that out and focus on other areas it shone.

That's a powerful sales message about the company you worked for, and remember, the better they look the better you look!

Don't worry if you've only worked for small companies. You don't know what the recruiter has been asked to find in an applicant. Even if the search is for a huge company, the hiring manager may be looking for small company background.

> *I was conducting a search for a client that was a top four international accountancy-consulting firm. They requested that I find a new Chartered Accountant from a small firm. I asked why; they certainly had the clout to pull a CA from any company, including their direct competition. The recruiter told me that at such a large firm, CA Auditors only get to see a small part of the process; they are responsible for one piece of the overall audit. At smaller firms, however, a CA student would often be responsible for the audit from start to finish, with intimate involvement in every part. So you see, this person would have an advantage over a large firm recruit. Sometimes smaller is better.*

Even small, anonymous companies can have areas at which they excel and graduates of such a work environment can be appealing… provided the recruiter learns of these things!

STEP 4e: Create a Company Synopsis for each prior employer (as shown on pages 151–152)

If you have another employer to add, remember, beyond your 3rd role, you can reduce and consolidate your Responsibilities section as older roles will likely be less relevant to a recruiter.

As you can see, it's growing well and everything we've added so far has been just what recruiters want to see. You can see here that you don't recognize **any** of the companies…yet by reading the synopses it's easy to be impressed.

Recruiters will be. Save the file and let's move on!

STEP 4f: Populate Responsibilities area with your own information

Use your **Responsibilities Done!** worksheet from Chapter 3 to fill in the duties you performed at the companies listed on your résumé. Use the most common and comprehensive listings of responsibilities from your saved lists; the ones that you found time and again on different job descriptions. Those will quickly resonate with a recruiter and you need to ensure they're there.

Consolidate your longer list into the bullet points available. If you came up with 19 responsibilities, group together the ones that can readily be combined and list them under one bullet. Aim for 8–12 in your most recent roles, and you can distill those from older positions to 5–7 points.

Follow the rules of Content. Powerful bullet points with strong action words detailing what you were hired to do will be noticed and appreciated.

Remember, the job descriptions you printed off to use here were professionally prepared by recruiters and hirers, so they will likely be clear and useful. They will not, however, possess the flair that you yourself could inject with newfound understanding of powerful bullets and action verbs. Make whatever changes you need to bring them to top form. Use the ones from those lists that match your experience and list those first, combining them with action. Don't forget to add your best to the list if they differ. Remember HR may not have **any** experience in your field so watch your words.

DAVID J. GARDNER MBA

1313 Mockingbird Lane, Toronto, ON, M4W 2H8

Cell: 416-389-4986

davidjgardner_sales@gmail.com

Core Competencies

Key strength
Key strength
Key strength
Key strength
Key strength
Key strength

Professional Experience

Sales Manager, THE TURKEY PALACE, Toronto   June '06–Present

International manufacturer/distributor of poultry products with stores in 15 major North American cities and average annual growth of 58% since inception (NYSE: TTPi)

Responsibilities:

- Responsibility
- Responsibility
- Responsibility
- Responsibility
- Responsibility
- Responsibility
- Responsibility

Accomplishments:

- Saved money/made money/process/awards/recognition

Senior Salesperson, ONCE AGAIN SUITS, East York   July '02–Feb. '06

Reseller/distributor/retailer of name-brand suits with $268M in annual revenue and 2nd largest in the industry

Responsibilities:

- Responsibility
- Responsibility
- Responsibility
- Responsibility
- Responsibility
- Responsibility
- Responsibility

Accomplishments:

- Saved money/made money/process/awards/recognition

(continued)

Sales Representative, PROMETHEUS CORPORATION, Toronto March '98–June '02
Manufacturer/retailer of eco-friendly batteries with distribution to 57 countries and sales in excess of $1.2B

Responsibilities:
- Responsibility
- Responsibility
- Responsibility
- Responsibility
- Responsibility
- Responsibility
- Responsibility

Accomplishments:
- Saved money/made money/process/awards/recognition

For example, in a search for a professional Sales Representative, job descriptions online produced the following common threads:

EXAMPLE: *Identify and resolve client concerns*

Work closely with customers to meet their needs

Seek out client problems and address accordingly

> *Applying for a position requires considerable skill. Research the role and show me why you deserve this role. What makes you stand out? Be objective and give me something measurable.*
>
> Dee Sharma— Director of Human Resources, CGA Canada

Worded differently, these responsibilities are actually similar in their need, concerned with solving client issues…obviously it's a key responsibility and so we need to include it. Here's another set of examples:

EXAMPLE: *Retain relationships to further sales opportunities*

Work to develop long-lasting customer relationships

Satisfy client needs to keep them happy and buying

This set describes another key responsibility.
Finally, in the Requirements section of the job description we found this focus:

EXAMPLE: *High level communication in English*

Superior spoken and written communication

DAVID J. GARDNER MBA
1313 Mockingbird Lane, Toronto, ON, M4W 2H8
Cell: 416-389-4986
davidjgardner_sales@gmail.com

Core Competencies

Key strength
Key strength
Key strength
Key strength
Key strength
Key strength

Professional Experience

Sales Manager, THE TURKEY PALACE, Toronto   June '06–Present
International manufacturer/distributor of poultry products with stores in 15 major North American cities and average annual growth of 58% since inception (NYSE: TTPi)

Responsibilities:
- Train, motivate, review, and promote 28 sales team members covering the entire East Region of Toronto
- Develop business plan to locate, connect with, present to, and close new clients through full RFP in a competitor-rich environment
- Provide timely, accurate, competitive pricing on all prospect applications submitted for pricing and approval, while striving to maintain maximum profit margin
- Set challenging top-down goals in line with corporate strategy for growth and profitability
- Full accountability for scheduling, metrics, sales and tax paperwork, staff desk efficiency and effectiveness, service levels, reporting, and new location scouting
- Present to top clients, senior management, at sales conferences and general meetings utilizing state-of-the-art presentation techniques
- Collaborate closely with Product, Finance, and Engineering divisions to ensure full cycle integrity from development to delivery and maintenance, ensuring client satisfaction

Accomplishments:
- Saved money/made money/process/Awards/recognition

Senior Sales Representative, ONCE AGAIN SUITS, East York   July '02–Feb. '06
Reseller/distributor/retailer of name-brand suits with $268M in annual revenue and 2nd largest in the industry

Responsibilities:
- Supervised, trained, mentored, and assisted in performance review of 5 Sales Representatives
- Created new clients and sales opportunities with cold calls, prospecting, attending conferences, networking
- Utilized powerful written and oral communication techniques to proactively identify and resolve client issues, ensuring 100% satisfaction and ongoing buying relationship
- Responsible for full cycle of sales from lead generation to sale to service follow up for self and staff
- Confidently delivered an explanation of product and service features and benefits, and the company's ability to deliver to customer expectations
- Monitored stock levels, evaluated product quality, tested service, and polled clients to ensure continual improvement in process

Accomplishments:
- Saved money/made money/process/Awards/recognition

(continued)

Sales Representative, PROMETHEUS CORPORATION, Toronto   March '98–June '02
Manufacturer/retailer of eco-friendly batteries with distribution to 57 countries and sales in excess of $1.2B

Responsibilities:

- Built customer base in assigned territory through cold calls, trade show and event participation, and all appropriate outbound sales activities
- Developed a strong understanding of customer's core objectives and challenges, in order to properly match the company's products and services with their needs
- Designed and delivered presentations and proposals as necessary to achieve success in given territory
- Kept efficient track of all leads, sales, contacts, and other information using LeadTrack to ensure efficiency and help management adjust metrics
- Maintained top level professionalism, punctuality, courtesy, integrity, and protocol in all interactions with clients and internal management

Accomplishments:

- Saved money/made money/process/Awards/recognition

So then, while we could list them separately, we chose to combine these three, all proven important to the recruiter, and deliver an effective single bullet point to list in our Responsibilities section:

> *Utilize powerful written and oral communication techniques to proactively identify and resolve client issues, ensuring 100% satisfaction and ongoing buying relationship*

Don't forget those action verbs and other rules of Content. Let's do it! (See pages 156–157 for sample.)

Save, and marvel at it. Remember, your responsibilities are packaged here in a compelling way, presented so that recruiters can best evaluate you as a fit. But they remain examples of what your role calls/called for, not what set you apart. You want to fit as much as possible in this area that qualifies you for your next position, but the way you set yourself apart is not listed in this section.

By now you're really starting to get the feel for this.

INSIDER SECRET

Applicants are paranoid that the slightest gap in work history, misstep in career path, or demotion will disqualify them. This is usually not the case. These can be overlooked if your résumé is great aside from this, but attempting to hide such things is rarely forgiven.

STEP 4g: Add your own selected Accomplishments to that section

Let's complete the Professional Experience section with the powerful Accomplishments subsection bullet points using the list we created in chapter 3.

Under each set of responsibilities, we will note approximately three key accomplishments you contributed at that job. Take your brainstormed accomplishments from Step 2e and choose your three most significant and insert them into your Master Résumé.

Remember, a company wants to know how you made money, saved money, or introduced or improved a process. Quantitative facts should be included here. Use percentages, dollar values, places, quarters, and numbers for impact.

A résumé is a document largely built with words, and so numbers stand out. 32% increase in new sales, $23,000 found in lost receivables, 'Outperformed quota 4/5 quarters', '14 new skus introduced with 12% market penetration' will all catch the attention of a recruiter. They want specifics where possible, and the Accomplishments section is the premiere showcase for your work achievements.

INSIDER SECRET

Compare your listed accomplishments to this example, which I've listed with the empty bottom fields as well. Do your accomplishments scream excellence? Do they begin with a powerful action verb? Can you put yourself in a hiring manager's shoes for a second and read it…would you be impressed? If not, go back and tweak it to bring out its best.

We've indented the Accomplishment bullet list a bit here to separate them visually from the vertical line created by the Responsibilities section.

Before we move on, save your résumé again. Do you see the balance that your formatted template is making possible as you fill in your responsibilities? Do you recognize the flow from one position to another? Even though the responsibilities and accomplishments differ, they read with the same ease and impact with the same potency. **This**

David J. Gardner MBA

1313 Mockingbird Lane, Toronto, ON, M4W 2H8
Cell: 416-389-4986
davidjgardner_sales@gmail.com

Core Competencies

Key strength
Key strength
Key strength
Key strength
Key strength
Key strength

Professional Experience

Sales Manager, THE TURKEY PALACE, Toronto   June '06–Present

International manufacturer/distributor of poultry products with stores in 15 major North American cities and average annual growth of 58% since inception (NYSE: TTPi)

Responsibilities:

- Train, motivate, review, and promote 28 sales team members covering the entire East Region of Toronto
- Develop business plan to locate, connect with, present to, and close new clients through full RFP in a competitor-rich environment
- Provide timely, accurate, competitive pricing on all prospect applications submitted for pricing and approval, while striving to maintain maximum profit margin
- Set challenging top-down goals in line with corporate strategy for growth and profitability
- Full accountability for scheduling, metrics, sales and tax paperwork, staff desk efficiency and effectiveness, service levels, reporting, and new location scouting
- Present to top clients, senior management, at sales conferences and general meetings utilizing state-of-the-art presentation techniques
- Collaborate closely with Product, Finance, and Engineering divisions to ensure full cycle integrity from development to delivery and maintenance, ensuring client satisfaction

Accomplishments:

- Grew territory by 35%, adding 3 new stores and 8 new corporate clients, recognized as the best performance of 2009 at Annual Sales Meeting
- Earned 'Gold Level' Performance status and awarded at Annual General Meeting
- Designed two new sales techniques which brought team sales up by 13% each quarter

Senior Sales Representative, ONCE AGAIN SUITS, East York   July '02–Feb. '06

Reseller/distributor/retailer of name-brand suits with $268M in annual revenue and 2nd largest in the industry

Responsibilities:

- Supervised, trained, mentored, and assisted in performance review of 5 Sales Representatives
- Created new clients and sales opportunities with cold calls, prospecting, attending conferences, networking
- Utilized powerful written and oral communication techniques to proactively identify and resolve client issues, ensuring 100% satisfaction and ongoing buying relationship
- Responsible for full cycle of sales from lead generation to sale to service follow up for self and staff
- Confidently delivered an explanation of product and service features and benefits, and the company's ability to deliver to customer expectations
- Monitored stock levels, evaluated product quality, tested service, and polled clients to ensure continual improvement in process

Accomplishments:
- ○ Innovated product display alternatives, doubling POP sales
- ○ Voted MVP of our city sales team 4 times
- ○ Utilized initiative to mentor 3 new junior reps, created morning 'Sales Blasts'

Sales Representative, PROMETHEUS CORPORATION, Toronto   March '98–June '02
   Manufacturer/retailer of eco-friendly batteries with distribution to 57 countries and sales in excess of $1.2B

Responsibilities:
- • Built customer base in assigned territory through cold calls, trade show and event participation, and all appropriate outbound sales activities
- • Developed a strong understanding of customer's core objectives and challenges, in order to properly match the company's products and services with their needs
- • Designed and delivered presentations and proposals as necessary to achieve success in given territory
- • Kept efficient track of all leads, sales, contacts, and other information using LeadTrack to ensure efficiency and help management adjust metrics
- • Maintained top level professionalism, punctuality, courtesy, integrity, and protocol in all interactions with clients and internal management

Accomplishments:
- ○ Created Community Battery Recycling Program endorsed by town councilor
- ○ 98% customer loyalty rating achieved due to superlative service
- ○ 20% average growth in my territory for 4 consecutive quarters

is what recruiters **love** to see…a shame most others don't do it, but **you** do and that's what will set you apart.

Let's nail down the remaining sections.

EDUCATION: Next, move down to the Education section and fill in each area over the generic ones we first entered as cues. The inclusion of this section is essential, but the formatting is less vital than the previous ones.

STEP 4h: Populate the Education section with your own information

List completed degrees and diplomas in reverse chronological format. If you are still quite new to the workforce and so lack extensive professional experience to fill up the remaining content, or if you have no post-secondary education, you should list your high school information here. If your GPA is considered high (over 3.0 of maximum 4.0), or if there is anything else noteworthy about the education you can list them.

Example for Junior Professional:

Education

Earl Haig Secondary School, Toronto, ON
Ontario Secondary School Graduate Diploma (SSGD)   2010
Enriched (Gifted) level in English, Math, and Science
GPA of 3.8
School Honor Roll 2 years

Although on the surface the Education section offers a reader little but cold scholastic facts, you can see how we can introduce highlights and accomplishments, again to set you apart. The chief lesson here is that ideally your experience speaks loudly for itself and you simply list your education. However, if your experience alone won't be powerful enough, then increase the potency and prominence of any and everything **else** with the same strategy of powerful bullets showing how you were 'above and beyond'. You may not get another chance to toot your own horn, so make it count.

Here's how my standard Education example turned out:

Education

York University, Toronto, ON
Bachelor of Economics Degree, B.Ec.   1996

Purdy straightforward!

COMPUTER SKILLS: In most cases this section is simply a list of your computer ability. You will provide the recruiter with a full record of which software programs, systems, and packages you have experience with, and your level of competence with each.

One excellent strategy for this section if you have stronger than average ability at a program is to let the recruiter know through ranking. It will be assumed if you list MS Excel that you have an average ability. But if your skill goes beyond this and you can program V lookups, pivot tables, 'If' statements, and even design templates using Basic coding, then you must list your greater competence level!

By highlighting *advanced* or *expert* level skill, you bring greater clarity, just what recruiters long to see, especially when their job description **requires** comfort with that program. While it's true that there can be a bit of inconsistency in how a recruiter interprets your listed competency level especially if these are not test-proven levels, categorizing your proficiency is undeniably valuable to them.

Familiarity—Have seen it, understand its basic nature and benefits

Beginner—Have used it, can navigate it, and use it at an elementary level

Intermediate—Average user, able to use it competently, can also be called **proficient**

Advanced—Power user with the ability to work quickly, comfortably, and knowledge of more complicated functions average users do not use

Expert—Highest level of use, often programmer level, or certified, or has been long time user with knowledge of every program facet.

If you have *intermediate* knowledge, then you needn't list it because that will be assumed. If you have *beginner* level, don't bother listing proficiency, just the software or system because it will reduce your overall résumé impact. If you operate at an *advanced* or *expert* level then you must include this as it sets you apart!

Also, although not for use in your Master Résumé, which isn't tailored to one individual job description, if a role specifically asks for 'skill in Powerpoint' for example, and you have only low-level exposure, make sure you list it! It will act as a keyword, and you are being honest. Just list it as 'familiarity with Powerpoint' in this section. The recruiter will want more information about your level of use, but it will be a positive as they evaluate you since you hit one of their job description list items.

How do you know which level you are? Many recruitment agencies that deal with entry-level applicants will be able to test you for free and let you know. It's a good idea to do it, as your chosen path may have strong needs in one area and if a test shows you lacking you'll know you need to improve your skills there. Tests online are also available if you dig for them. If you are a more experienced professional, just use the list above to evaluate your own level. Unless that skill is a dealmaker or breaker it won't matter.

If you have many skills in this section, be sure to highlight the ones relevant to your career path first. So our fictional professional fills out like this:

Computer Skills

Oracle, Hyperion
Proficient in Leadtrack Plus and SAP
Advanced proficiency in Word, Leadtrack V1.0, Powerpoint, and Excel
Familiarity with Prophet

The format for listing here is not vital but the content is.

STEP 4i: Populate the Computer Skills area with your own information

Fill your Computer Skills area as detailed above and save the file.

STEP 4j: Populate the final sections with your own information

With the most important areas covered in detail, continue down your résumé, filling in the listed areas as they come up. They are already formatted well, and so simply use your experiences and choose which you can and want to include and exclude. Take note of the information in the **Format** chapter while listing your experience, and here are some additional tips.

Professional Development: Pull these from your Chapter 3 notes and fill in the section. If you are a junior professional, be more liberal in what you include. More seasoned pros can be more particular, including the most relevant first. If your role is one wherein ongoing development is encouraged but not mandated, a strong Professional Development section alone can separate you from your competitors!

Publications/Presentations/Patents: A clean listing such as this adheres to our format well. Note that if you have no patents, for example, leave that part of the title off. Again, take the experience from your notes and plug it in to your Master Résumé.

Publications/Presentations

- 'How to sell well', 1998 published in *Big Company Newspapers*
- 'Marketing Top 10' 2004 published in *Marketing Monthly*
- *'How to Raise the Bar and Sell like Mad'* presented to each new sales team 2003–2008

AFFILIATIONS, MEMBERSHIPS, CERTIFICATION, LICENSES, ASSO-CIATIONS, TRADE ORGANIZATIONS, MENTORSHIP, VOLUNTEER-ISM: List these if relevant or if you need to flesh out an otherwise lean résumé due to lack of experience. Be careful of the possible perception of your involvement. Political, religious, and controversial groups may be a proud part of your life but you must measure it against its impact. If you are a member of the Martian Abduction Society of Upper Manhattan, that **may** create an opportunity for a recruiter to prejudge you, even when it isn't their intent. Our example:

Memberships & Licenses

- Member in Good Standing of the CPSA (Canadian Professional Sales Association)
- Affiliate Member of NASP (National Association of Sales Professionals) in Michigan, USA
- Licensed Poultry Sales Consultant since 1996

Languages: As with Computer Skills, list languages along with your level of competence in each. If a job description specifically asks for a particular language, emphasize your competence by stating that you have advanced ability or, ideally, are fluent. If you have only a basic understanding, it likely won't be relevant. Remember, you needn't list English. Also, if you have a certification of level in language proficiency, list it here.

Languages

Fluent in written and spoken French, Spanish, and Intermediate spoken Japanese

Awards/Honors: If there are awards and honors that have not been included in the Accomplishments section of your résumé, then include them here. If you have the space, this is an excellent opportunity to show the recruiter that you are outstanding. Even if there is some lack of outward relevance, quality recognition is an example of your being a superior candidate.

THE OTHERS: For the 'Doesn't matter' areas, should you choose to include them, follow the formatting and content rules already laid out to retain a sense of balance and cleanliness on your résumé.

Done. Save your file!

Core Competencies

Now we have created the résumé proper, we have the necessary information to go back and design your **Core Competencies** list.

If your résumé is your professional life in a couple of pages, the Core Competencies section is the very same information distilled to about 6–8 points. Not only is this the synthesis of everything you are professionally, but inclusion of a robust profile not only helps the recruiter quickly gauge your pedigree, it also increases your searchability. The myriad bots used by search engines on the Internet, and logarithms and parameters used in recruitment by company Applicant Tracking Systems all key into the presence and number of appearances of relevant skills and experiences, positively affecting your rating.

STEP 4k: Determine which Core Competencies are most powerful and add

Carefully scrutinize your résumé, the responsibilities you've been accountable for and accomplishments you've achieved. Decide upon 6–8 areas in which you shine. This group should be a concentration of both hard skills, such as technical ability, and soft skills, such as people management. Depending upon your field and its focus on the technical versus people sides, you can adjust the ratio of hard and soft. In most cases for junior professionals emphasis is on technical ability because one might lack the leadership and other people-related skills common in higher-level roles. For these entry-level individuals a 6:2 or 7:1 ratio favoring the technical is best. For mid to high level professionals, up the ratio to 5:3 or 4:4 depending upon the role and, as mentioned, the field.

Here's how our Sales Manager appears with the Core Competencies included. You can see we brought together some of the listed attributes under the Leadership tag:

<u>Core Competencies</u>

Leadership—Award-winning management with big picture, enterprise-wide mindset and 8+ years leading teams from 4–28 employees to success

Performance—Average 12% increase in sales each quarter over 12 years

Growth—Steady, controlled overall regional growth of 6% including during industry downturn in 2008 recession

Retention—92% employee retention utilizing mentorship, encouragement, inspiration, and a 'Player's Manager' mentality

Improvement—Creator of over 10 new initiatives embraced nationally, improving lead generation, organization, demonstrations, closing ratios, and back end sales

Technical—Superior computing and systems skills, advanced ability in numerous sales related performance optimization packages

Of the six listed above, Leadership and Retention would be soft skills, and Performance, Growth, and Improvement, would be considered hard skills. Remember, your list will contain the core areas key for you. Even if you're a Sales Manager yourself, your list may look very different from our example.

Now that all the sections are filled in, here's how it looks (see pages 165–166). Keep in mind that this is a sales résumé and the optional sections may differ somewhat.

Now that you have it done, let's move on to the essential tightening, nipping, and tucking that most people either ignore or are ignorant of and bring out that final sparkle that is a reflection of the perfection we've been striving to achieve.

Fine Tuning

You're not done. As great as it looks right now, builders of the best résumés add an important next step: the fine tune. They edit, shape, edit, proofread, edit, give it to another to evaluate, and, oh yes, **edit.**

Start by opening your résumé and reading it **as a recruiter** might. Look at the general job descriptions for your career path, and imagine that you are a recruiter looking for someone to call for an interview. Keep a few things in mind:

- You are busy, so a clear, clean, readable résumé will help you read it and get what you need fast

- You have pressure from hiring managers, so strong bullet points, powerful quantitative facts, keywords matching job descriptions will help qualify a contender thoroughly

- You don't just want a warm body, so it has to be someone more than ordinary to join your great company. So you want to see how this person saved money, made money, implemented or improved a process

- It should be well-balanced, with a kind of symmetry in the number of responsibility points, accomplishments, bullet types, fonts, sizes, and white space

Looking at the résumé in front of you as a recruiter, would you be impressed? By now your résumé is far beyond the 85% of résumés in the poor to good range, and we just need to tighten it up to ensure that it gets beyond great to that top 5% of résumé excellence.

STEP 4l: Carefully edit your completed résumé

Go through the following areas and tighten up your résumé through careful editing.

Spelling and usage. Go through the résumé and check every word, correcting for spelling and the way it is used in the phrase. Word by word…it shouldn't be more than about 700-1,000 words at two pages…take your time. Read it out loud in order to catch usage errors.

David J. Gardner MBA

1313 Mockingbird Lane, Toronto, ON, M4W 2H8
Cell: 416–389–4986
davidjgardner_sales@gmail.com

Core Competencies

Leadership—Award-winning management with big picture, enterprise-wide mindset and 10+ years leading teams from 4–28 employees to success

Performance—Average 12% increase in sales each quarter over 12 years

Growth—Steady, controlled overall regional growth of 6% including during industry downturn in 2008 recession

Retention—92% employee retention utilizing mentorship, encouragement, inspiration, and a 'Player's Manager' mentality

Improvement—Creator of over 10 new initiatives embraced nationally, improving lead generation, organization, demonstrations, closing ratios, and back end sales

Technical—Superior computing and systems skills, advanced ability in numerous sales related performance optimization packages

Professional Experience

Sales Manager, The Turkey Palace, Toronto   June '06–Present

International manufacturer/distributor of poultry products with stores in 15 major North American cities and average annual growth of 58% since inception (NYSE: TTPi)

Responsibilities:

- Train, motivate, review, and promote 28 sales team members covering the entire East Region of Toronto
- Develop business plan to locate, connect with, present to, and close new clients through full RFP in a competitor-rich environment
- Provide timely, accurate, competitive pricing on all prospect applications submitted for pricing and approval, while striving to maintain maximum profit margin
- Set challenging top-down goals in line with corporate strategy for growth and profitability
- Full accountability for scheduling, metrics, sales and tax paperwork, staff desk efficiency and effectiveness, service levels, reporting, and new location scouting
- Present to top clients, senior management, at sales conferences and general meetings utilizing state-of-the-art presentation techniques
- Collaborate closely with Product, Finance, and Engineering divisions to ensure full cycle integrity from development to delivery and maintenance, ensuring client satisfaction

Accomplishments:

- Grew territory by 35%, adding 3 new stores and 8 new corporate clients, recognized as the best performance of 2009 at Annual Sales Meeting
- Earned 'Gold Level' Performance status and awarded at Annual General Meeting
- Designed two new sales techniques which brought team sales up by 13% each quarter

Senior Salesperson, Once Again Suits, East York   July '02–Feb. '06

Reseller/distributor/retailer of name-brand suits with $268M in annual revenue and 2nd largest in the industry

Responsibilities:

- Supervised, trained, mentored, and assisted in performance review of 5 Sales Representatives
- Created new clients and sales opportunities with cold calls, prospecting, attending conferences, networking
- Utilized powerful written and oral communication techniques to proactively identify and resolve client issues, ensuring 100% satisfaction and ongoing buying relationship
- Responsible for full cycle of sales from lead generation to sale to service follow up for self and staff
- Confidently delivered an explanation of product and service features and benefits, and the company's ability to deliver to customer expectations
- Monitored stock levels, evaluated product quality, tested service, and polled clients to ensure continual improvement in process

(continued)

Accomplishments:
- ○ Innovated product display alternatives, doubling POP sales
- ○ Voted MVP of our city sales team 4 times
- ○ Utilized initiative to mentor 3 new junior reps, created morning 'Sales Blasts'

Sales Representative, PROMETHEUS CORPORATION, Toronto   March '98–June '02
Manufacturer/retailer of eco-friendly batteries with distribution to 57 countries and sales in excess of $1.2B

Responsibilities:
- Built customer base in assigned territory through cold calls, trade show and event participation, and all appropriate outbound sales activities
- Developed a strong understanding of customer's core objectives and challenges, in order to properly match the company's products and services with their needs
- Designed and delivered presentations and proposals as necessary to achieve success in given territory
- Kept efficient track of all leads, sales, contacts, and other information using LeadTrack to ensure efficiency and help management adjust metrics
- Maintained top level professionalism, punctuality, courtesy, integrity, and protocol in all interactions with clients and internal management

Accomplishments:
- ○ Created Community Battery Recycling Program endorsed by town councilor
- ○ 98% customer loyalty rating achieved due to superlative service
- ○ 20% average growth in my territory for 4 consecutive quarters

Education

University of Manitoba, Winnipeg, MB
Masters of Business Arts Degree, MBA   2008

York University, Toronto, ON
Bachelor of Economics Degree, B.Ec.   1996

Computer Skills

Oracle, Hyperion
Proficient in Leadtrack Plus and SAP
Advanced proficiency in Word, Leadtrack V1.0, Powerpoint, and Excel
Familiarity with Prophet

Publications/Presentations

- 'How to sell well', 1998 published in Big Company Newspapers
- 'Marketing Top 10' 2004 published in Marketing Monthly
- 'How to Raise the Bar and Sell like Mad' presented to each new sales team 2003–2008

Memberships/Licenses

- Member in Good Standing of the CPSA (Canadian Professional Sales Association)
- Affiliate Member of NASP (National Association of Sales Professionals) in Michigan, USA
- Licensed Poultry Sales Consultant since 1996

Languages

Fluent in written and spoken French, Spanish, and Intermediate spoken Japanese

The Internet can be a useful tool in proofing. Better yet, however, ask someone professionally skilled in written English communication.

- Check for overall balance. Pin the résumé to a wall and take a step back. Is it busy with words? Is there too much white space? Is it a pleasant balance of content and white?

- Check the fonts. There should be just **one** type. Have you used bold, underline, and italics attractively, without going overboard? Do they adhere to a hierarchy of size that is consistent?

- Check the bullets. Are they all from the same bullet family?

- Check tabs and alignment. Are all dates in the same vertical line? Are all first bullets lined up? If you needed to do subsets of bullets within bullet groups, are they lined up?

- Scrutinize your word choice. Are your phrases succinct, yet full of meaning? Will the recruiter and their software key in to your terminology?

- Tense. Present if you are still working at a company, and all else past.

- Sentences. **No sentences.**

- Personal pronouns. No.

- Colons/Semicolons. If you used them, have you followed the rules?

- Articles. You should have deleted most of them, but not so many as to leave a phrase without its meaning.

- Adjectives. Have you included any meaningless, self-aggrandizing fluff?

- UPPER CASE. If you have chosen to use it, does it contribute TO your résumé by giving a uniform accent to something, or detract by SHOUTING?

- Abbreviations. Do you know the right ones? Have you used them correctly?

- Verbs. Have you thought carefully about every powerful, action-oriented verb?

> *I find modifications needed in over 80% of résumés I receive. Formatting, spelling, large fonts, fluff, bulky vague descriptions, and absence of relevant stats!*
>
> Sean Armstrong— Recruiting Specialist, Wheels Group

STEP 4m: Make adjustments to alter length if required

Length. The final adjustments—While it's true that the rules for résumé length have loosened over time, attaining that goal of a neat and orderly product requires careful editing for length. Whether you aim for a two or three page résumé, your aim should be **full** pages. You may need to edit down to shrink a bit, or up to expand, but a résumé wherein each page is as full and complete as the others is the rule. Here's how you can make small changes to shrink or grow your résumé to fit page length.

Font size: A subtle shift up or down in size can do a lot to affect page length. If you need to eat up more space to grow your content, try upping your font size by 1. Remember that if you do it for one part, you must do it for all and the size hierarchy must be adjusted. As stated earlier, you don't want your font too small as it will affect readability. Also, too large gives a reader the sense that you have less experience and are trying too hard to fill space.

Line Spacing: A better bet is to make some small changes to your line spacing. Paragraph or simply line spacing can subtly affect length without detracting from visual appeal. In fact, sometimes tighter spacing can improve readability as it brings relevant sections in close and removes them from following sections. **Caveat:** Be consistent. If you reduce line spacing too much it can remove tops and bottoms of letters. Increasing spacing can give an effect of disconnecting sections that should be kept together.

Margins: The best option for making some adjustments to page length is the increase or reduction in top, bottom, left, and right margins. Try a combination of both to make the effect less noticeable. If your résumé runs a touch too long, open up the top and bottom margins first. The default may be set at about 1 inch or 2.54 cm. Dial this back to .9 inches and see what happens to the résumé content. You can go to about .5 inches either side, but don't go beyond that or you will risk being conspicuous. If your résumé is too short, you can increase the margins to 1.4 inches, but no more than that.

Left and right are set at .98 inches or 2.5cm. Try not to mess around with these unless the top and bottom adjustments are working by themselves.

Having said all of this about page length, if you simply cannot effectively hit the 2 or 3 page mark on the button, and end up with 2 ½, so be it. Tight pages are great, but if it would mean throwing off size and balance and content to the degree that they suffer, it isn't worth it. Also, in many instances your résumé will look off on another's computer screen. So long as it **prints** out to the tight 2 or 3 pages, you're set.

STEP 4n: Proof your résumé thoroughly

The final step: Ugh. I **hate** to have people look at my work for mistakes. I mean, I'm an English teacher, specialist, and writer…my English is perfect.

Not at all!

All reputable authors of **any** writing style and media rely upon someone else to at the very least proofread their work. Regardless of your background or level of professional development, I cannot emphasize enough the importance of having someone qualified review your résumé for errors.

Within your circle of friends and acquaintances there is likely a proficient English expert. Ask them if they wouldn't mind reading over your résumé for **spelling and word usage.** Don't ask them to evaluate it, make changes, or give you advice on content; they're not qualified. They will feel compelled to help you craft full sentences and they will be off-put by the abruptness of your punchy professional pedigree. Print them a hard copy and ask them to make notes in red pen detailing spelling mistakes and usage errors only. If they ask you why you don't just spell check in your software suite, tell them you don't trust it, you trust them. They'll be thrilled.

You may be surprised to find that despite your careful scrutiny of the résumé, this English pro finds an error or two…or more. It happens to us all, and aside from their qualifications, giving someone an opportunity to proofread this important document also simply provides a fresh set of eyes. It's absolutely worth it. Do it. Either they will correct

> *Ensure your résumé is grammatically correct and doesn't contain any typos—it is amazing how many people do not proofread their résumés! For me, it demonstrates lack of professionalism.*
> Brenda Brown—
> Sr. Vice-President
> of Human Resources,
> Compass Group
> Canada

something, which helps, or they won't be able to find any errors, meaning you are an outstanding self-editor…either way you win.

C'est ca. Your masterpiece, the Master Résumé is complete! Let's move on to a necessary sibling of the résumé, the cover letter, and then wrap up with the 5th and final Master Key to the ultimate résumé.

Chapter 6 Summary

Chapter STEPS

STEP 4a: Create your Master Résumé document file

STEP 4b: Populate the Contact Information with your own personal details

STEP 4c: Populate the Professional Experience area with your own information

STEP 4d: Create a Company Synopsis from your Chapter 3 notes

STEP 4e: Create a Company Synopsis for each prior employer and save the file

STEP 4f: Populate Responsibilities area with your own information

STEP 4g: Add your own selected Accomplishments to that section

STEP 4h: Populate the Education section with your own information

STEP 4i: Populate the Computer Skills area with your own information

STEP 4j: Populate the final sections with your own information

STEP 4k: Determine which Core Competencies are most powerful and add

STEP 4l: Carefully edit your completed résumé

STEP 4m: Make adjustments to alter length if required

STEP 4n: Proof your résumé thoroughly

There's nothing worse than a generic cover letter. If you don't take the time to write ME (the recruiter, the role, the company), why would I take the time to read it for YOU?

Nicole Bradfield
—Placement Group Recruiting

chapter 7

The Cover Letter

Here's another surprising insider insight into a commonly-accepted job seeker belief: Not only is your cover letter **not** read first, but **at least 25% of the time it's *not read at ALL!***

Unfortunately, you're not off the hook...you still need one.

A cover letter was originally intended to be an introduction for an applicant and their résumé. It covers the résumé as a first document, and is written much more in the customary business letter format. Some job-hunters, facing the intimidating task of building a top-notch résumé without help, perhaps because they feel the résumé they have in hand is not impressive enough, turn the majority of their time and effort to the cover letter. This, they feel, is the best way to fully express their candidacy since the résumé can seem cold and lifeless.

Terrible mistake!

It's called a cover letter, but the more accurate and current description is a *backing letter*. In fact, it doesn't introduce your résumé, as was its original role, now it's the other way around! When a recruiter receives your cover letter and résumé, they will almost always skip right to the résumé. The quality of your résumé will give them an indication as to whether or not they should even bother with your letter! If your

> *I read them only after I've read the résumé. If they look like a fit or someone of interest I go back to the cover letter.*
> Brian Drake—
> Sr. Recruiter,
> David Aplin
> Recruiting

résumé is poor, or even fair, it isn't worth reading your cover letter. If it can stand under that initial scrutiny, there is a growing chance that they will read your entire submission.

RÉSUMÉ SUCCESS 600 SURVEY HIGHLIGHT

Over 20% of all submitted résumés come without a cover letter.

Because your Master Résumé, and each focused résumé you will submit to specific jobs going forward will be seen as first-rate in quality, your cover letter **will** be read and so you need to do it right.

INSIDER SECRET Unless your résumé is great enough for them to consider you as a possible hire, they won't bother reading your cover letter.

Despite its relegation to a supporting role, the complementary cover letter does require a high standard of quality to work well. Unfortunately, the lion's share of applicants who do submit a letter fall into a couple of common traps that render the document useless.

The most common error is the generic submission. Bland in content and general in coverage, the one-size-should-fit-all cover letter is far from what a recruiter wants. I need only read a few lines of such a document and I can readily tell that the writer is not addressing **my** company's needs, arguing a fit with **my** job description, but instead has sent a fluffy catch-all letter that convinces me of little except that they didn't take the time.

Less common but equally frustrating to a recruiter is the arrogant cover letter. Rife with empty, self-aggrandizing boasts and unproven pronouncements, this document turns off in a challenge to a reviewer that says, 'if you don't hire me you're a fool because I'm **spectacular**.'

Many other poor variants exist, trying so hard, yet missing their mark.

Is it possible for a quality cover letter to actually add more to the overall submission, strengthening the résumé and overall submission?

Yes. So long as you understand what a cover letter is really used for, and help it fulfill its need.

Like the résumé, the cover letter has different purposes depending upon which side of the recruitment table you sit. Understand, however, that while you feel that there are several important things to get across in your cover letter, the recruiter is using it to screen you in or out based upon those things **plus** many more! The cover letter can be a valuable tool for the recruiter to continue to evaluate a candidate's appropriateness for a role in their company.

> *Yes, I read them. I like to see the writing style and quality. Often they are riddled with errors, which tells me a huge amount about that candidate.*
> Jeff Aplin—
> COO, David
> Aplin Recruiting

The Applicant Uses a Cover Letter:

- To introduce your résumé
- To explain any gaps or possible questions that will arise from reading your résumé
- To express interest in the company and role applied to

The Recruiter Uses a Cover Letter:

- To find explanation to gaps and questions they have after reading your résumé
- To find out why you are interested in their company
- To discover why you are interested in the vacant role specifically
- To evaluate if you fully understand their needs
- To learn why you feel qualified for the position
- To reflects your overall level of professionalism
- To evaluate your English communication skills
- To look for sincerity and earnestness
- To learn about soft skills not included in the résumé
- To get a feel for your personality and character and to judge if it is a good fit for their organization
- To discover the best ways, times, and methods to get in touch with you

The cover letter indicates the personality and passion of the writer.
Nelson Chan—
Recruiting Manager,
Compass Group

In order to construct an **excellent** cover letter, it's important, as with the résumé, to take the recruiter's needs seriously. Regardless of what you want to tell them, don't ignore **their** needs!

I have experienced the cover letter disconnect first hand as a recruiter. I have received, read, and trashed tens of thousands of them! The rest of the **Résumé Success 600** vented identical frustrations. When asked **why** they choose to read or not read a résumé, recruiters answered with a great deal of uniformity:

RÉSUMÉ SUCCESS 600 SURVEY HIGHLIGHT

Top 5 Reasons recruiters choose 'YES' to reading a cover letter:

1. **Communication Skills.** Recruiters want to know that you can write well! They will check for spelling issues, format consistency, professionalism, grammar, use of language, and ability to convey a persuasive argument for your candidacy.

2. **Reason for Application.** They want to know why you applied. What led you to their website? Why would you leave your current employer? Why do you feel you are a good person for the role?

3. **Personality.** They want to get to know you. Because the résumé possesses a necessary cold, fact-based aspect, recruiters read cover letters to learn about the person you are. They study your passion, attitude, values, beliefs, and overall personality.

4. **Are You Paying Attention?** Recruiters want to know that you are applying to their specific company and position. Not much is more frustrating to a recruiter than to open a cover letter and find it's either generic drivel or worse, not even addressed to their company. This is how they can get an idea if you are committed to **their** organization, or if you're spamming yourself all over.

5. **To Answer a Résumé Question.** When a recruiter finds a gap or inconsistency in your résumé, they will want a reason for it. Such things must be explained in the cover letter, and not the résumé proper.

When asked what they discover most often and dislike most about cover letters, the **Résumé Success 600** group responded uniformly:

Top Recruiter Peeves about Cover Letters

- **Generic.** Not specific to my posted job with relevant matching points
- **Simple errors.** Some applicants leave other company names on letter heading, spelling errors, poor grammar.
- **No Direction.** No intent or substance. It's wordy without actually saying anything.
- **No personality.** So bland on the one side or officious on the other that they couldn't get a sense of the real you.
- **Length.** Too long or short. They don't have time for 2+ page cover letter. One short paragraph isn't enough.

So we see the reasons for cover letter review are quite clear, but what do they really want from you? If they could wave a magic wand and let you know just what they love to see in your cover letter, what would it be?

I asked the **Résumé Success 600**, and here's what recruiters would **love** and be thrilled to read on your cover letter…and they rarely see.

What top recruiters say makes a *great* cover letter:

- **Reason for Application (Why You Are Interested):** Recruiters want to know what made you decide to apply. Is it one of 50 applications you spammed out? (hint: *wrong answer*) Have you heard great things about their company and were awaiting an opening there? Does something in their company, industry, or job description resonate with you…compel you to apply? (hint: *right answer!*)
- **How Your Experience Benefits Their Company:** they don't just want to know what you've done, they've seen that on the résumé; they want to see how your previous experience will fill their need, suit their purposes, fulfill their expectations. If you had started your own company and grown

(continued)

RÉSUMÉ SUCCESS 600 SURVEY HIGHLIGHT *(continued)*

it in the past, you must help the company realize how your entrepreneurial determination and drive will benefit them. Make it relevant.

- **Your Future, Goals, and Career Path:** They want to know that you won't outgrow them, and that your dreams are in line with their development. They want to see if you are a professional match, that you suit their corporate culture, and that your mission and values are aligned.

- **It's Personalized:** You should try to use the recruiter's name if possible, and absolutely use the company name, correctly.

- **Highlights:** Using the Core Competencies, Responsibilities, and Accomplishments sections on your résumé, give them some powerful facts about what you bring to the table **as it relates** to what they are looking for. You don't want to simply regurgitate the highlights. Again, make them relevant.

- **Communication Skills:** Unlike the résumé that has some of its own rules of grammar, the cover letter should include the standards of English with the exception of numeration, which we covered. From spelling to grammar, sentence form and flow, to capitalization and abbreviation, this is not the place to compromise your ability to communicate. A recruiter wants to know not only that you can communicate in English, but also that you have competence to the degree that you can use it persuasively in a professional environment. It should reflect a strong grasp of your English, but not so business formal that they can't identify the real you. Watch your tone, which should be friendly but not too chummy. Confident but not arrogant.

| **INSIDER SECRET** | Avoid sterile 'proper' business letters. They are efficient and correct, but lack personality. Recruiters want to see your character in the cover letter you send them. Be polite, respectful, and thoughtful…but be *you*. |

- **Customized:** Throughout the cover letter you should be referring to what they look for in their job description. If you have a strong knowledge not only of the role, but also of their company, you will in the construction of your cover letter increase the degree to which you match what the recruiter

(continued)

RÉSUMÉ SUCCESS 600 SURVEY HIGHLIGHT (CONTINUED)

is looking for. If, for example, their website seems to focus on strong growth above other goals, make certain you refer to your experience and interest in growing business. Also, the more customized to the exact job description, the higher your rating on the search by their Applicant Tracking System. The program cannot usually separate résumé from cover letter and so scans both together for keywords.

- **Contact info and availability:** Be very clear about when and how to reach you. Help them manage their expectations surrounding your ability to get back to them. If you pick up your messages only once a day, tell them you will respond within 24 hours or sooner. Let them know when you are available for interviews. If they know, they can accommodate you, if not, they may get frustrated at your seeming lack of follow up and move on to another candidate.

- **Layout:** It must be neat, clean, and easy to read. They want information, but they want it to be in a form that isn't a nightmare to wade through. Block format aligned left, with a standard font and 4-6 paragraphs or reasonable length will increase readability.

- **How you heard about the job:** Part of a recruiter's job is to market the role on job boards, on the company website, at fairs, and many other places. By letting them know how you found the opening, you help them evaluate their marketing. Never forget: helping them helps you.

- **Do you understand what they want:** Recruiters often find that applicants will send their résumé to every open position even close to their experience. This is, you must realize by now, a patent waste of time. While reading your cover letter, they will interpret your understanding of their requirements. If you have a strong grasp of your field and their needs, you will hit the mark. If you speak in generalities and don't address their requests, you aren't their next hire.

- **Why you are leaving your current role:** If you are currently working, you can let them know why you would consider leaving. Put a positive spin on it. If you don't have the confidence to do so, leave it off and deal with it in interview. If you are not working at present, let the reviewer know why you

(continued)

RÉSUMÉ SUCCESS 600 SURVEY HIGHLIGHT *(concluded)*

left. Avoid the stronger words such as fired, and instead, use downsized, restructured out, laid off, as it applies to your situation. Unless you were let go due to wrongdoing or incompetence, it's fine to include and won't detract from your candidacy.

- **Organized thought process:** A cover letter, like an essay, has flow. It transitions from one argument or thought to the next easily and with conviction.

  When economical uses of word count are important, each phrase should be carefully chosen and contribute to the introduction, argument, and closing of your document.

- **What makes you different:** Just as the accomplishment section of the résumé separated you from the also-rans, recruiters want you to come right out and let them know **why YOU?** Remove yourself from the pack with specific and quantifiable reasons why you are the right person for the role.

This is what recruiters say would make your cover letter an absolute winner. Let's then, use it as a framework for what must be included in your own creation. You may be feeling a bit intimidated by the volume and specific information required in your cover letter to bring it to that top 5% in your field. Don't worry, we'll break it down and make it easy to manage!

Let's refer to our 5 Master Keys and apply them to the cover letter:

Knowledge: how you heard about the job, understanding what they want, why leaving current role, why you are interested

Format: layout, short and concise

Experience: the benefit to their company of your experience, your interests past, present, future, highlights, what makes you different

Content: communication skills in writing

Submission: contact info and availability, personalized, customized

It's no surprise that the same key areas that can make your résumé an elite document can also, according to recruiters, bring your cover letter in line with what they are thrilled to read.

> A cover letter or résumé that reflects a lack of political correctness can end your candidacy immediately. PC will be assumed so be careful. Use gender-neutral, non-judgmental, apolitical, unprejudiced language.

INSIDER SECRET

We must construct a cover letter that contains each of these aspects.

Here is a chart reflecting how a much weight a recruiter will place on your résumé and cover letter in getting you a call or interview based upon its quality:

A great résumé—	a great cover letter	- ALWAYS
A great résumé—	a fair cover letter	- ALWAYS
A great résumé—	a poor cover letter	- LIKELY
A good résumé—	a great cover letter	- LIKELY
A good résumé—	a fair cover letter	- MAYBE
A good résumé—	a poor cover letter	- MAYBE
A poor résumé—	a great cover letter	- NEVER
A poor résumé—	a fair cover letter	- NEVER
A poor résumé—	a poor cover letter	- NEVER

You can see that while the **résumé** is the most important indicator of whether or not you will be contacted for interview, the cover letter **does** contribute.

Unlike the résumé proper one cannot create a clear template for a cover letter because it has too many individual variables depending upon what you bring to the table. We can, however, come close, including each aspect recruiters love to read and leaving little room for error. Look at the following example on page 182.

This letter example encapsulates each aspect that recruiters want, and, as the top résumés do, brings a cover letter to that top 5% versus

No, I don't usually read cover letters, unfortunately, because they're all the same. 'I'm looking for a challenging opportunity to use my unique skills to make a significant contribution to a grow- ing com- pany…blah, blah, blah'. Generic and useless to me.
Greg Ford—VP Talentclick

David J. Gardner
123 Willow Drive
Toronto, ON M3E 4W3
416-315-5588

Friday January 12, 2010.

Attn: Recruiter for Marketing Manager role (ID: 343)
Green Acres Markets
154 Caledonia Ave
Toronto, ON M3W 4E3

Dear Recruiter;

As an accomplished senior marketer with over 15 years of progressive skill, I was thrilled to discover your need for a highly skilled Marketing Manager on your website. I have visited the site numerous times in the hopes of finding an opening with you, as your core values of community, leadership, and environmental stewardship mirror my own beliefs so closely. My ability to attract customers from challenging demographics, develop innovative strategies, and my absolute passion for my field seems very much a fit for your posted role. Your need of someone to lead a sizeable team and introduce new models for product presentation is an outstanding mirror to the successes I have accomplished in prior roles and coincide with my current employer's relocation of our local operation out of country.

At Excel Marketing I was hired to rejuvenate print advertising and remedy a stagnant market share, which I accomplished with a new flier design and price adjustments that resulted in a 14% increase in brand recognition and 11% increase in sales. Although they are a union environment, as is Green Acres, I used diplomacy and empathy to create a bridge between workers and management, resulting in a decline in worker absenteeism, increase in morale, and boost to productivity. At Brigantine Foods, I worked extensively on product placement within stores, introducing a point of purchase (POP) display system that reverse a decline in sales and resulted in a 4% increase.

Prior to my time at Brigantine I took a year to further my education through two marketing courses, and travel extensively. I attribute the success of my career so far to my ongoing commitment to learning, improving, and a sincere love for marketing. I have a deep desire to grow long term with a company such as Green Acres, well recognized for grooming senior talent from within; I am certain my contributions will reflect my worth.

I so very much appreciate the time you have taken to review my application. I kindly request a meeting to discuss how I can help Green Acres not only continue its success, but move beyond to greater profitability. I can be reached at the above cell number any time daily, 7 days a week from 6:30am-8:00pm, and return calls within the hour. I am available to interview immediately. I look very much forward to hearing from you!

Very sincerely,
David J. Gardner.

the competition. Yours will be this length **or shorter.** I deliberately added extra information such as a gap to be explained and extra quantitative accomplishments to illustrate the potency of such a structure. Should you need to expand the margins slightly you can do so, but beware of clutter.

Let's build it. You can see the below steps reflected in the above example for reference.

Note: *Below represents the closest we can come to a Master Cover Letter. Due to the highly subjective nature of its content relative to your particular background and desires, only coverage of the correct ingredients, sections, and flow can be taught here.*

STEP 5a: Create a cover letter document file

Open a new Word document, and leave the settings on their defaults. Save the file in this format: **'firstlastname_cover_companyname.doc'.** In my example then, **'davidjgardner_cover_greenacres.doc'** works well. Starting with your name shows consistency with your résumé document name, and helps a recruiter keep your information together. Sometimes your files will get separated as the recruiter moves them, copies them, and imports them, so they'll appreciate your organization. The reason you might want to abbreviate 'cover letter' to 'cover' is to provide room for the important company name. Having the company in the file name not only gives the reviewer the correct impression that you are personalizing the submission to them specifically, but in your own computer the files will be easily searchable and so before the interview you can review what you had sent to them for consistency sake.

> *Be sincere and present who you really are, not who you think you should be to get the position. Research the organization and be passionate about what you can contribute to its success.*
>
> Nicole Bradfield— Recruitment Consultant, Placement Group

Keep your cover letter to one page, approximately 250 words. Keep the sentences succinct and the paragraphs no longer than 3–5 sentences. This is the ideal length.

INSIDER SECRET

STEP 5b: Enter the address and date information first on your letter

You will use the formal block style formatting, meaning you won't indent the first part of any paragraph, and you won't right align addresses, dates, or signatures.

If you choose to use tab alignment, then move the date, your address, and your bottom name at the same vertical point on the page as you see in the above example.

Justification is more customary here, as it creates a neater, crisper appearing document. However, ragged right style is also acceptable.

You can use the default Times New Roman font, or the same font you used in the résumé itself. This differs slightly from some business letter formats, but it is well recognized as a strong format and set up for cover letters.

Enter your contact information at the top as you see in the correct example. Enter name, address, and contact information just as it appears on the résumé.

Go down two spaces and enter the date in full

Another two spaces and enter the company information. For the time being if you don't know to whom it should be addressed, enter 'Attention: Recruiter for _____ position'. In the Submission chapter we will detail how you can get this information. Below that list the company and its address. Be sure to spell the name of the company correctly. Save the file.

STEP 5c: Enter the appropriate salutation

Salutation. Down another two spaces, begin your letter with 'Dear Recruiter'. If you have been able to get a name for this person, enter it here. If the company lists a reference number or code for the posted role, include it here to aid them in organizing your application.

STEP 5d: Create the introductory paragraph

Paragraph 1—Introduction. In this section you let the recruiter know where you learned of the open position and why you are applying.

Yes, I read the cover letter. It shows that the candidate is interested and has done their homework on the position that they applied for.
Matt Bateman—Recruiting Manager, Compass Group

The former helps the recruiters identify where their own marketing efforts are having an effect. Whenever possible, refer to the listing of the job from their company website and not a general job board. You want them to know that you're targeting **their** company. The latter, the reason for your application, is an important piece of information to a recruiter. They want to know what it was that led you to writing the letter and submitting your résumé. They have a need; do you think you can fill it? Was it the company? Was it because you've done all the role asks for already? Is it the location of the place? Do you know people who work there and love it? The more professional and personal affinity you have for a position at that company, which led to the application, the better. If you've been referred to the role by anyone working there, make sure you include their name! Referrals from internal sources can absolutely help. In some ways this is a teaser paragraph, setting the stage for the next section.

Avoid the common mistake of making the focus of the cover letter all about *you*. You highlight yourself only so that you can let them know how you will improve their company. It's really all about *them!*

STEP 5e: Continue the cover letter with your experience and skills

Paragraph 2—Experience and Skills. Likely the longest paragraph of the cover letter, here you will give powerful evidence of your overall professional fit for the role. You may choose to use bullet points here, but do not simply take them from your résumé; the recruiter does not want your letter to be a reiteration of the information they've already read. It should be specific to the role you are applying for whenever possible, so use their terms. Why are you the person to fill their needs? What makes you different? What do you bring that makes you the right fit? How have you made money, saved money, or introduced/improved a process that will benefit this company? You may need to break this into two paragraphs to avoid unappealing length.

> **INSIDER SECRET**
>
> In cover letter as in interview, show interest in the company and the role! Show passion for your profession! Far from fluff, a genuine love for that which you do works wonders in a cover letter.

STEP 5f: Continue the cover letter with your goals and additional information

Paragraph 3—Goals and Others. In this paragraph you will include whatever left you have in your arsenal you haven't used yet. Are there other skills or talents you feel will benefit the company? Importantly, what are your goals in the long and short term and how are they in synch with the company? Were there any gaps in your résumé that need to be explained?

STEP 5g: Conclude the cover letter

Paragraph 4—Close and Follow Up. Here you wrap up the letter with several important points. You thank the reviewer for taking the time. This may seem like a bit of polite fluff, but if done sincerely it does help because they **are** busy. You also want to ask for the interview! In sales there is the term 'the close', referring to the point at which one asks for the completion of the sale. Many salespeople do a fantastic job of educating the customer, but then don't bother to ask for the sale! Many recruiters want to see that confidence, so long as it's done without arrogance or assumption. Tell them why you are their best man/woman. Finally, you must provide detailed information on the best way and times to contact you, and when you are available for interview.

Some additional tips on how to create an outstanding cover letter:

Take the features and benefits tack: A feature is a fact and a benefit reflects what the fact **means** for them. For example, in a car, a **feature** might be 6 airbags. The **benefit** of having airbags means never having to worry about the safety of your loved ones as you drive. A feature of a local pharmacy is that it's open 24/7. The benefit is that you can get your medication anytime, any day you need it. On your cover letter, a feature of your experience may be a recent professional designation, but a benefit to a new employer may be that they can be reassured that you bring current, relevant industry knowledge to their team. This is an effective technique you can use.

No personal information: Showing your personality and additional information about your character is not the same as opening up about your personal information. Beliefs, hobbies, age, marital status, even salary information and reasons for leaving positions can hurt your chances, so don't include them.

STEP 5h: Save, print, and thoroughly proof your cover letter

Save your file. Print out a copy and proofread. Just as you did with your résumé, let a competent person you trust read your cover letter. Take a step back from it and look at the page. Does it look like a handful, chock-a-block full and a challenge to read? Or is it broken down to digestible chunks, and clean and clear to read?

Read your résumé again as a recruiter: There will be questions in the mind of the recruiter after reading your résumé. Determine what these might be and address them in the cover letter.

Use their language, not yours: Remember that it likely won't be a hiring manager who first decides if you make it to interview. That first massive cut of applicants is by the recruiter, who is **not** in your field (unless you are an HR professional). Avoid jargon unless the words you are considering are very common in your area. If you use an abbreviation you'd be best to spell it out afterwards. Also, recruiters use words such as 'fit', and 'corporate culture'. Make sure you let them know that you are a good fit for their company. It's a comfy word for them and whether they realize it or not they'll soften a bit.

When you print: For job fairs and interviews you will need to print out a number of hard copies of your cover letter. Ensure that you use the same paper as your résumé for consistency. At a job fair, have the cover letter stapled in front of your résumé (yes, they'll read the résumé first but it's still protocol to have the cover on top). At interview, you can paperclip the two together so that the recruiter can easily slip it off to take notes without bending or tearing any part of your submission set.

> *Your cover letter needs to show your enthusiasm for the role for which we are recruiting. Keep your language simple and try not to use industry specific jargon.*
> Patti Clarkson—Staffing Advisor, Canadian Pacific Railway

That's it! That is all you need to know and do to create a cover letter that will greatly improve your chances of an interview. Next, let's get back to our Master Keys, and wrap up with an aspect of job-hunting that the majority of applicants neglect. The **best** way to get your professional message out there: The Submission.

Chapter 7 Summary

- The cover letter is not read 25% of the time
- The cover letter is actually read after the résumé, and only if the résumé is good enough

Applicant Uses Cover Letter:

- To introduce résumé
- To explain gaps and answer questions
- To show interest in role

Recruiter Uses Cover Letter:

- To have gaps explained
- To find out why you're interested
- To Discover why you want this specific role
- To learn if you understand their needs
- To read why you feel you are qualified
- To discern your level of professionalism
- To Evaluate your communication skills
- To gauge your sincerity and earnestness
- To uncover soft skills not on résumé
- To get a feel for your personality and character
- To find out your contact and scheduling information

- Recruiters hate résumés that are generic, contain simple errors an edit should catch, lack direction and personality, and are too long or short
- A great cover letter can help your application but without a great résumé it is rendered useless
- Cover letter sections:
  - Salutation
  - Introduction
  - Experience and Skills
  - Goals and Others
  - Conclusion and Follow Up

Chapter STEPS

STEP 5a: Create a cover letter document file

STEP 5b: Enter the address and date information first on your letter

STEP 5c: Enter the appropriate salutation

STEP 5d: Create the introductory paragraph

STEP 5e: Continue the cover letter with your experience and skills

STEP 5f: Continue the cover letter with your goals and additional information

STEP 5g: Conclude the cover letter

STEP 5h: Save, print, and thoroughly proof your cover letter

A résumé should be considered written advocacy; all portions of the application work together (résumé, cover letter, correspondence) to convince the recruiter to grant an interview.

Mary Jackson
—Chief Officer, Legal Personnel
Blake, Cassels, & Graydon LLP

chapter 8

Master Key #5: SUBMISSION

Now that you have the best possible documentation to represent your professional reputation, we turn to the challenge of getting it out your door and into the right hands.

Keys to a successful application involve a number of things. It's not as easy as visiting a job board and sending your résumé...**everyone** does that. With some strategic planning and tact, you can ensure that your résumé and cover letter are in the best place and the best time to provide you with the very best opportunities.

Every submission route you use has the same goal. To get your résumé in front of the most relevant person at the company you want to join. **Direct application, recruitment agencies, job boards, networking, and job fairs** represent the most common methods you can utilize to reach that goal.

Tailoring your Master Résumé: The Focus Résumé

When submitting using these methods, you will sometimes provide your **Master Résumé.** When you aren't aware of the specific needs of a role or company, you will always default to this form. Don't be concerned that it remains a little generic at this point. It is far superior right now to almost any other résumé circulating in your field.

At other times, and whenever possible, you will use your Master to create what's called the **Focus Résumé.** It's here that we use the job description and other available information to fine-tune your résumé to be a direct fit for what the company has outlined as being important for their organization, and specifically, the posted role. This is the laser we spoke about earlier that vastly outperforms the standard shotgun résumé. And, as promised, it won't take much time, especially considering its potency.

With your Master Résumé open, my file name being **'davidjgardner_sales_resume.doc',** take the description for the specific position you want to target and read it thoroughly. Each and every aspect listed is valuable to that company for whoever is hired for that role. Go through each responsibility listed, line-by-line. Consider where in your career you have carried out that responsibility, and go to the relevant section on your résumé, altering what you had listed to be a closer match for the new role.

For example, you are a Sr. Financial Analyst and read in a job description for Green Acres Markets (where you'd love to work) that they're looking for a candidate with 'experience with ERP *(Enterprise Resource Planning) implementation'*. You have that experience from a few different companies, but you've only listed it once in a bullet point detailing, 'Demonstrated strong computing ability with weekly mentorship of new hires, upgrades, and an ERP implementation'. This point is strong for your Master Résumé as a catchall about your system savvy, but now you know that Green Acres Markets is interested in that specific ERP point.

You must buoy to the surface **all** the corresponding experiences and skills you have relating to that on your résumé. So you re-jig that bullet to read, 'Spearheaded ERP package implementation from concept, procured buy-in from executives, and completed 2 months ahead of demanding schedule'. You are fleshing out the experience, improving it specific to the description here. If you had such experience at other companies, you would also bring that out and showcase it.

STEP 6a: Create a Focus Résumé document file

Because this résumé is specifically focused on this one role, save it as a file with the company name in it. **'davidjgardner_resume_greenacres. doc'** or similar will help your job search organization, and is professionally adroit as a recruiter will see that you specifically entitled it with their name. When you recall the cover letter file is **'davidjgardner_cover_ greenacres.doc'**, you can see the consistency…consistency that will aid a recruiter and indicate your organization and professionalism.

Imagine that as the recruiter scans your résumé, every time they find an item listed on their job description that you have highlighted, a green light goes on. The more green lights, the closer a fit you are for the role in their eyes. Once enough green lights illuminate, they **will** call you.

Also, if they are using their Applicant Tracking System, the more your résumé reflects the job description your 'hit rating' will buoy you to the top of their search list! Your job is to take every part of the job description, be it 'Responsibilities', 'Qualifications', or aspects of character or personality they need, and bring it out in your résumé. With a thorough 30–45 minutes you can easily bring your alignment with a posted position from a 7/10 (which is the closest most generic résumés get), to a 9 or 9.5.

Never allow dishonesty to creep into your résumé as you detail your match for the role, however. The idea behind the success of a strong Focus Résumé is that you have quality experience and education enough, but the job description and company website allow you to move from a good match to a perfect one.

> *Résumés should tell a story and give the reader a window in to the journey you are on professionally. If the story is well written and tailored for the job you are seeking, the recruiter is likely to want to speak with you.*
>
> Meldon Wolfgang— Managing Director, The Boston Consulting Group

Less than 1 in 20 applicants use a Focus Résumé. This is one of the most *underutilized* ways to have a recruiter love your experience as it compares to their posted position.

INSIDER SECRET

Direct Submission to a Company

Direct submission is the most straightforward method of getting your résumé to the recruiter responsible for deciding if you get an interview. Through submission via email, a web portal, or online application page set, your information is sent directly to the decision-maker.

Advantages

- No middle-people separating you from internal corporate review

- The company will save money by not paying a recruitment agency fee and so if they feel they've got a quality lead they **will** call

Disadvantages

- No middle-people to filter, educate, and help you follow protocol with inside information

- If you make a mistake in your submission it could mean exclusion from the process

There are two instances in which you would submit your résumé directly to a company.

Job Specific application: You identify a company in your city at which you would love to work. You go to their website and find in their Careers/Jobs section that there is a position open in your field and it looks like a good fit. You apply to it then and there.

In this method you use a Focus Résumé to align your experience most closely with what they are asking for in their job description.

Company General Application: Let's say that you identify a great company in your city. Perhaps it's on the 'Top 100 Best Companies to Work For' list, as are most of the companies that assisted in the research for this book. If there is no position that is a fit for you, you can call the company and let them know you would like to submit your résumé to keep on file should something come up. Recruiters won't want to be pestered, but most companies will have a Human Resources email to which you can send your résumé without directly applying to a specific role. Check the website first for this link! They won't be happy if you called in and the email address is clearly indicated on their site.

If you choose to submit this way, then you may elect to make few changes to your Master Résumé. It is already prepared to be a great fit for any company looking for qualities generally required for your area of specialization. You should thoroughly scrutinize their site, however, and if they show a clear interest in a certain type of person, like lively and fun, or a skill, such as recently trained, you should make sure that's reflected in the résumé you submit. It won't be a complete Focus Résumé, but many aspects of it will deliberately coincide with what they look for in a new employee. **Every** slight increase in your fit compared to what they want is a step closer to being hired.

Recruitment Agencies

When evaluated and handled correctly, recruitment agencies can be extremely powerful allies in finding your next great job. Think about it…their full time role is to find companies that need to hire and work tirelessly to find the best people for those roles. If you are sent to interview at a company by an agency recruiter, you are already shortlisted. They can be like your talent agent, a career mentor, résumé advisor, interview coach, and person-on-the-inside.

Advantages

- Often have access to jobs that aren't advertised. A client company may let them have a go at filling a role before it is made public.

- Can offer advice on résumé, interview, and help you manage your expectations.

- They will know much more about the company you are being submitted to, such as corporate culture, salary, who the players are and what their personalities are like.

- If they don't find the right person for an open job, then they don't get paid. This can be a great incentive for them to work with you to get you ready to submit and beyond, to interview and offer stage.

- Sometimes they will have an exclusive or semi-exclusive agreement with the company, meaning that **only** they will provide people to interview and be hired. That narrows your competition a great deal.

- They are often very qualified at résumé review. Company recruiters are specialists at determining what their company likes, but agency recruiters have multiple clients, and deal with a myriad of qualifications by different companies. They must be adept at identifying top qualities in résumés and what their companies value.

- After being sent to an interview with a company, the recruiter can give you valuable feedback they receive from the company recruiter to help you improve.

- Great recruiters will work with you long-term, placing you more than once in your career and keeping in touch with you, providing you valuable marketplace intelligence, and letting you know what's out there.

- If you are a great applicant, recruiters can even market you into great companies regardless of whether there's a position there or not.

Disadvantages

- All are **not** created equally. Many firms are volume machines, treating people like cattle, cutting corners, and doing whatever it takes to close the deal.

- They may use information you provide them to solicit business not in your best interest, e.g., asking you where you are interviewing and then calling that company so they can try and fill that role with other applicants.

- They are always busy, and may not respond to your calls or email.

- They may coerce you into accepting a lower salary, or lowering expectations to get an offer signed.

- They may say they represent you, but you don't pay them, their real allegiance will most often be with the client company.

- They can be fair-weather friends. When things go poorly at a client interview, they may just move on and not help you going forward.

- The industry is metrics driven, meaning success in the business is a numbers game, and a certain number of interviews with them is expected by their boss. They may be interviewing you to meet a quota or just to boost their personnel inventory so that in the future they may call you and many like you en masse.

Should you use agency recruiters? Absolutely! The advantages are just too significant to ignore. The challenge then is to know how to use them best, without compromising your professional integrity.

Just as with direct submissions to companies, you can submit two ways to a recruitment agency:

Job Specific Application: You visit the agency's website and see a role that looks like a great fit for you and apply directly to it. They will call to screen and book an interview, or reply to your application by email. Should your résumé not be a good fit and still strong in general then they will keep it on file for consideration for future opportunities. Sometimes they will bring you in regardless, based simply on the strength of your résumé. Later, when something comes up that's a match, they can simply call you, tell you about it, and forward your résumé to their client company instead of waiting to book an interview with them first.

Agency General Application: You many not see a role that they agency is representing that is a great fit at present. If you have heard good things about the agency and feel there might be a good opportunity for a working relationship, you may want to submit your résumé to the recruiter sourcing for your field in their office, and not to a specific role. See below for strategies on submitting yourself to a prospective agency with no specific role in mind.

Here are some tips on how to successfully find and manage agency recruiters:

Locating A Good Recruiter

Find 7–10 recruitment agencies in your city and meet with them. Agency recruiters don't meet just anyone, but your résumé is now top caliber and regardless of whether or not they have a role right now that alone will give you a great deal of credibility.

Use the Internet to find agencies that cover your 'space' or 'vertical'. Some agencies recruit for many different fields, but others may work specifically with your area of expertise. You'd be surprised at how niche-focused agencies can be. If you're in sales management and you approach a recruitment company that only deals with accounting professionals, it's not going to help you.

Even if there isn't a relevant position for you, ensure that they pay attention to your talent. Remember, their main focus will be on applicants for their existing open positions. Use the following techniques to get them to call you:

- Reply to a position posted on their website that's a good fit for you. Follow up with a call to make sure they got it. They will likely call to do a phone screen, and if that goes well, an interview.

- Call in to reception and introduce yourself. Reception may not let your call through to a recruiter but they should be able to give you the name of a recruiter you can send your résumé to.

- Most agency websites will have the phone numbers and extensions of recruiters listed. Call them directly.

If they answer, briefly introduce yourself and ask if you can send your résumé. Brief means brief! They're very busy. 'Hello (use their name!), my name is David Gardner and I'm a Sr. Engineer in the greater tri-state area. *I'm considering moving to a new company and wonder if I can send you my résumé?*' Get the email address (although you'll likely already have it), and say you'll send it along shortly. Once you've sent your résumé, follow up the next day with a call to make sure that they've gotten it.

If they don't answer when you first call, leave a message much like the brief introduction above. Don't give them too much information and always speak clearly and with a smile on your face. Tell them you'd like to send your résumé but don't have the address, and if they could give you a quick call to give you that information you'll send it along right away.

Reach out to the Manager or Vice-President of the recruitment agency, introduce yourself and ask whom is best to speak with. Show your initiative. This is most often an easier route into an agency than through the reception gatekeeper, who may suggest a generic email submission. It will be the responsibility of that person to ensure you and your résumé get into the right hands. If an executive sends one of their recruiters your résumé and asks them to contact you...you can be certain they will!

INSIDER SECRET

If they don't contact you or respond at all, move on. Your résumé will be imported into their Applicant Tracking System and if something that matches your skills comes up, they will call.

If you submitted your résumé online to a job posting, you may see that it's been posted by a recruitment agency. At this point you may not know which company it is they're representing. Apply to it. If your résumé is a fit they will contact you soon to discuss and set up an interview.

If you posted your résumé online, recruitment agencies commonly 'scrape' résumés to add to their system. Scraping means pulling your information from an external source and adding it to their ATS. You may be a match for a current position, and they'll call you, or perhaps they like your general background but don't have anything right now.

The Phone Screen

Some agencies will simply call you to book an interview, but others will first evaluate you through a phone screen. They don't want to waste their time, or yours, if you're not a fit. **Their goal** for the phone screen will be either to screen you specifically against a job description, or just to ensure your communication is up to snuff before they bring you in. **Your goal** for the phone screen is to get the face-to-face interview. The strength of your new résumé will go a **long** way to paving the path to an in-person meeting.

Tips for the Phone Screen

- Speak clearly and at a good volume

- Make sure there are no distracting background noises on your end

- If you are on your cell and the signal is weak, continue on a land line

- Smile. Smiles can be heard in your voice and people are naturally attracted to people smiling and are put at ease

- Be succinct in your answers—don't ramble

- Tell them that you will only be working with 2–3 recruiters and would like to meet to see if you can work together. This connotes exclusivity and they will appreciate your candor and that you understand how it works

- Ask them what you should bring to the interview and how you can best prepare for it

Your Meeting with A Recruiter

INSIDER SECRET

Your meeting with an agency recruiter is an interview. Regardless of how casual they may sound on the phone, or whether you head in to their opulent corporate office or grab a coffee together at a café, it is a bonafide interview. As such, you should make sure you dress the part. For most professions, that will mean business formal attire. Some professions are more casual, but always default to conservative business attire. If you're worried, you can always ask the recruiter. 'Since this is an interview, I'll be wearing a suit and tie, is that all right?'. This shows that you respect the process and gives them the opportunity to ask you to dress down if that's their preference.

Many applicants disrespect the agency recruiter interview by dressing casually, showing up late, not being groomed appropriately, or not appearing organized. This is a death knell for your job search. While highly qualified professionals are absolutely necessary for an agency recruiter to get paid, that doesn't mean that **you** are absolutely necessary. If you show up late, disheveled, unorganized, or unprepared, why on earth would they trust you in front of their esteemed client company?

Treat the agency interview with high respect, impress the recruiter, and they will in turn represent you very well.

In essence, you want to be an 'A' candidate.

Being an 'A' Candidate

What is an **'A' candidate?** In the world of recruiting, we generally relegate candidates, companies, and open job orders to **'A', 'B',** or **'C'** levels. Recruiters work most diligently on **'A'** job orders with **'A'** companies and send in **'A'** level candidates.

An **'A'** candidate has a fantastic résumé, interviews well, understands the hiring process, takes feedback well, is easy to work with, returns phone calls quickly, dresses appropriately, and if they're working on a specific role, fits that role closely.

Even if you are not a fit for the role they are currently working on, quality recruiters always keep **'A'** candidates close because they know they can trust them to perform well in a submission to a client company. **'A' candidates are place-able candidates.**

At the meeting with a recruiter, the agency may ask you to fill out a questionnaire or release form allowing them to possess and use your information on your behalf. This is all fairly standard.

Going into your meeting with the recruiter you must keep in mind that they are not paid by you, they do not work for you, and likely have a number of others equally qualified standing by or waiting in their email inbox. The key to working successfully with agency recruiters comes from grasping this, and doing everything within your power to being an active partner in your relationship. Make their lives easier and they'll work on your behalf.

The interview itself may come in many different forms. Some agency recruiters flash through a set list of questions in 20 minutes, and others can take over an hour and a half. Beware of fast interviews as they are often a reflection of a volume shop. You may be one of 6 interviews set up for that day. A quality interview can be had at 45 minutes to an hour. Some may ask behavioral questions such as **'tell me about a time when ___ happened, and how you handled it.'** Others may have a form and move from the general to the specific about your career and goals.

Some Areas You Need to Make Sure They Cover

- Your salary expectations
- Reasonable commute to work
- Long term goals
- Environment (culture) you enjoy working in
- Detailed history and successes
- When you are available to be sent to interview
- Best way to contact you
- Most important things to you in your next role
- Your ability to relocate and under what circumstances
- Your references are prepared
- Position titles you would next accept

I consider these to be basic coverage for an interview. If they **only** want to know if you can do 'x' and 'y', because their client company demands that, then they aren't going to be able to represent you well. If they don't know your full picture, they may simply consider you for anything and send yourself and a small army of other applicants to every job they represent, hoping any one of you get the role. The volume submission by agencies is, unfortunately, fairly common and disrespects the hard working professional recruiters who send a short list of their top people to a company expecting one will nail it and the others will be very close.

Take your own list of questions to the interview. While they are interviewing you for a current or future position, you are also interviewing them! Your professional brand name is important, so you want the agency recruiters to whom you entrust it to be well qualified and trust-worthy. You can let them know that before you leave you have a number of questions to cover with them. They'll either be impressed and respect it, an indication of a quality recruiter, or they'll be off-put and hurry through them because you've passed over their allotted time for you. If this is the case then they probably aren't worth your time as well.

Preface the questions by letting them know that you only plan to be represented by 3 recruiting agencies and you want to make sure it's the right fit for both sides.

Questions for a Recruiter

- How long have you been recruiting?
- How long have you been with this company?
- Who are your company's top corporate clients?
- Do you have exclusive arrangements with any of them?
- Have you placed people there?

If there is a specific role that you are interviewing for:

- Have you personally placed any people at this company?
- Have you been to the company?
- Have you met with the corporate recruiter there?
- How many people will you be submitting to them for this role?
- Are you exclusively representing this role or are other agencies working on it?
- When might I expect feedback on my candidacy for this role?

You needn't have them written down if you don't want, you could take a pad and paper and just jot notes as you inquire.

Be respectful and let them guide the interview! These are absolutely the right kind of questions to ask, but because not many applicants understand agency recruiting they won't expect you to ask them. Also, these questions are not yes/no accept/reject inquiries; you want to get a feel for them professionally. If, for example, they have not placed anyone at that company, it doesn't disqualify them. It just contributes to your overall idea of them.

Of course, also be honest.

When finished and wrapping up, be sincere, warm, friendly, and thank them for their time with a handshake and a smile. Tell them you look forward to hearing from them and ask if there's anything you can do in preparation for the possibility of moving forward. Ask them what next steps are. Ask them also what the best way to keep in touch is, email or phone. They will have a preference. If there is no specific role that you're being considered for, ask if you can follow up in a couple of weeks.

Choosing and Following Up

Evaluate them based upon their interview and follow up. The firm they work for may be a reflection of their ability to help you. Big firms may have more professional clout, but may be a volume shop. Small agencies may have close relationships with hiring managers and know intimately what they look for, but not much breadth of client base to support your full needs.

INSIDER SECRET

Instruct a recruiter to *never* submit you for a position without discussing it with you first. Good recruiters will do this anyway, but if you've accidentally gone with a cut-rate volume recruiter they may send your information to a company quickly just to make sure that the submission credit goes to them and not another agency. They can be your search partner but it's *your* professional career at stake, so you must be apprised of everywhere your résumé goes. Company recruiters will assume that their agency counterparts are on the up-and-up and have asked you...but it doesn't always happen.

You can always ask recruiters what they think of other agencies. This is always fun, and you may gain valuable insight into either the agency you're sitting with, or the one mentioned. As a rule during my interviews I never dropped a company name when discussing volume shops or unethical firms, but I found that oftentimes the applicant brought it up, already having suffered disappointment at their hands.

Bad service has a loud voice.

Follow your gut. Choose three recruiters with agencies and make them your personal marketing force. If you choose to go with too many, they will place less interest in you. Exclusive or near-exclusive access to you professionally should be a privilege for a few only. Keep them close, update them on your progress and listen to their advice. Be kind and thoughtful to them and they will keep your résumé on their desk and work hard for you!

Job Board

A job board online is an electronic version of the old job boards you see at local employment offices, or in municipal centers. They provide searchable lists of a multitude of available positions posted there by companies and recruitment agencies on behalf of their corporate clients. Although there are just a few easily recognizable job boards representing the entire country, there exist a plethora of smaller boards catering to more specific job parameters. Some focus on higher bracket incomes, others only on marketing professionals...some deal specifically with one industry niche. The best way is to simply do an Internet search for job boards and check them out.

A job board is an access point for you in two ways: Firstly, you can search for potential job matches for you as posted, and even proactively keep you up to date on what's out there. Secondly, you can post your résumé there so that recruiters can find you readily.

The first incarnations of online job boards individually represented themselves and their particular clientele. However, in recent years powerful Job Search Engines have become the new normal. These complicated systems send their bots around the Internet to find job postings from virtually every source. They pull or scrape the postings and bring the link to their own site, which acts as a launching area for you. As a result, you can visit just a couple of major engine sites and have access to an overwhelming number of positions that match your criteria. You can enter 'Sales Manager', and 'Toronto' and it will find all the roles in the Greater Toronto Area that match your title, or have it contained in its description. Most have advanced search capabilities so that you can get very specific as to what will qualify a role for you. Clicking on a posted role will take you to the site of the company or agency representing it, and ask you to either fill out an online application, profile, or submit your résumé and cover letter, just as you would if you visited their sites directly. The one advantage here is that you can have access to numerous roles in your career area all in one place.

Many of these sites will also allow you to post your own résumé there. Not only do companies post their own jobs to see who will apply, they pay these sites for membership, allowing them to search for posted résumés by professionals such as you. In this way, they have a greater chance of finding the right person. If you haven't looked at the role they have available, they may find your résumé, call you, and invite your application.

Job boards are an extremely popular way of hunting for your next professional step. There are caveats, however, such as the fact that your posted résumé must be general because you're not aware of exactly what a prospective company is looking for, and that it makes public your personal information.

Job Alerts can be a useful tool as well. On a job board, or even at the career web portal of a sizeable company, you can sign up to receive an email anytime a new opportunity is posted that fits your selected parameters. These are highly recommended, and make sure they are sent to your new job search email address so that you can keep them organized.

Advantages

- Many jobs in one location
- Easy to follow links to submit
- Can post your own résumé for others to find
- Can often set up job alerts so that if a new role fits your parameters you receive a notification email

- Some may let you save many different profiles or versions of your résumé, assisting with customization

- Putting your résumé online means that it's accessible by potential employers 24/7

Disadvantages

- Can't tailor it to a specific role

- Detailed private information is made available to anyone with a subscription

- Dilution of your brand name through common access

- Sometimes submitting your profile means populating their often-inferior résumé templates

- Such powerful search engines and the volume of postings often leads to multiple submissions or spamming of your résumé

Networking

An alternative way to get your résumé in front of a prospective new employer, and possibly to the top of the pile, is by knowing someone. Gathering quality contacts in your industry, and in life as a whole, can help.

It is also the most commonly *misunderstood* method of Submission.

I recently came across the following generalized statistics about hiring patterns in North America:

Networking results in approximately 50–60% of hiring. Agency recruiters account for about 20–30%, and traditional Internet submission, less than 10%.

The information is not so much incorrect as grossly misleading. People mistakenly believe that if they attend mass networking sessions that opportunities will fall miraculously into their lap. In truth, the percentage of hires that take place due to each of these submission/introduction methods are **directly representative of the time required to have success with them.**

It takes the **least time** to have success with traditional submission techniques, as you find a role, create your Focus Résumé, and submit. It must be the mainstay of your search efforts.

It takes **more time** to have success with recruiters, as there are additional interviews, screenings, and evaluation of their companies/ competencies/commitment. It will complement your direct submissions, and, once you partner with top-notch recruiters, augment your submission potency.

INSIDER SECRET

> Be absolutely certain your reference will give you an honest, but *glowing* review. I've seen it happen far too often that a previous employer talks a recruiter out of going forward with a keen applicant.

It takes the **greatest amount of time** to have success with a network, especially if you are starting now. The reason is simple: knowing someone does not necessarily get you an **'in'** to a wonderful new job. Pressing palms, collecting business cards, or attending 'pink slip parties' represents only the first step in the lengthy process that culminates into a legitimate network. Networking is, in fact, the most powerful overall submission strategy, but it can take years to galvanize your group into the real advocates you will require. They must not simply know you, but trust you, respect you, and believe in your personal and professional brand in order to open their trusted doors to you.

If I meet you at a mixer and you ask for an introduction to a friend of mine who may be hiring, that could help…but the connection is weak, and my referral will be similarly so. If I have known you a while, however, and have a strong bond of mutual respect with you, have seen evidence of your professional or personal worth…and if I have grown to like you, that referral to my friend will be heavily weighted in your favor. Those are the connections that lead to consistent placements over an entire career.

So when is the best time to start and actively build and solidify your professional network? When you began your career.

When is the next best time? Right now!

Companies would **much** rather deal with a known quantity, and since recruiting efforts are expensive, having someone referred by an existing employee is a win-win situation. If you know someone at a company you have interest in, put it in your cover letter. Drop the name when you are phone screened or meet with them in interview. Better yet, have the contact give the introduction for you.

More and more, employers find it useful to enter an applicant name on a search engine to learn more about them. Make sure your accessible information is clean and professional!

Internet Networks: You can find online groups that are focused on your area of expertise such as professional affiliations that have meetings, or at minimum discussion boards online to share information. If you become a regular and respected member, someone may tap you on the shoulder and let you know that their company is hiring. A name helps, even if the reference only knows you a little, so long as the contact is positive it can help.

There are also more general **professional networking sites** online that allow you to provide some profile information and connect with others. One of the most popular at present is **LinkedIn.** As your list of contacts grows, it multiplies exponentially because with every new connection you gain some form of access to their contacts as well. LinkedIn has over 50 million connected users at the time this book went to print, and growing. Advice for LinkedIn users is to populate the professional profile section only with information you don't mind sharing. The inclusion of your professional history is standard and reflects a poorer form of a résumé. However, sections such as Recommendations, which are respected referrals, and other opportunities for personal branding make LinkedIn a worthwhile addition to your networking arsenal. Beware of unsolicited agency recruiters and unknown entities attempting to connect with you; they could be after your network and not your talent. Whenever you question their background as it relates to you, write a note to them before allowing the connection.

Using your **social networking site** profiles does not help you get a job. A prospective new employer doesn't want to head to your profile page to not only find your résumé and assorted professional information, but also photos of your drunken game of horseshoes up at the cottage or get an e-gift from you. Keep the social site for your social life and the professional one for your career development. You should do a search on your name online and see what results. Don't think that potential new employers won't use a search engine to see if something interesting comes up.

A professional network can absolutely open doors. It takes time and effort, however, and you still must be respected at what you do. If you have none, start your network now and nurture it for future use.

Job Fair

A job fair is not usually the **best** place for a seasoned professional to find their next employer, but it can help. For more junior job hunters, the job fair is a great place to be exposed to a large number of potential employers all under one roof.

The majority of job fairs are elaborate affairs, often taking place at convention centers and decked out with a bedazzling array of displays, posters, booths, stages, and swag. Companies, associations, and various groups looking to hire or attract talent to their professional industry or organization will attend and vie for new recruits to meet, screen, and consider. And many, many, many recruits **do** show up. It can be a bit of a madhouse.

If you want to make the most of a job fair, keep the following in mind:

Visit the fair website. Even smaller fairs may have a site to visit to get information. Check for presentations that may be valuable to you. Most importantly, have a look at the list of companies that will be represented there, and visit their websites to gain valuable intelligence there! It's impressive to a recruiter when you meet them at the fair and you know and understand their values.

Be prepared. Bring a stack of clean Master Résumés to provide to the company recruiters who will be working booths there. Also, dress appropriately! There may also be company brass in attendance, and if a recruiter wants a brief interview screen with you, or to introduce you to a manager, you'd be smart to look your best.

Schmooze. Job Fairs are fantastic places to meet new people relevant to your job search and network. Here you have a room full of recruiters, **all anxious to talk with you!** Collect business cards. After you've had a chat with someone and received their card and moved on, make a little note on the card, something that you learned about them in your chat. Make the rounds and be friendly and polite, confident but not arrogant. Remember the firm handshake, eye contact, and smile that represent a great first impression.

Follow up. You will be submitting your résumé to many companies there potentially…but remember, think about it from their perspective. You may walk out having given out twenty résumés and spoken with thirty recruiters, but the company recruiters may have met hundreds of applicants and have a huge stack of résumés to wade through back at the office. What people have had success doing with me is to call soon as soon as they got home. They knew I wasn't in the office, so they left a pleasant message about how wonderful it was to meet me and they'll resend their résumé right away so that I have an electronic copy of it (how thoughtful!). When you do this, use the email address on their card and send them a brief note. Thank them for spending the time to chat with you, slip in the bit of information you learned about them (*'I was impressed that you've been at __ for 14 years and still love it so much!'*), and attach your résumé again. At the very least they can add you to their ATS for future reference. Don't be a pest; they will be impressed that you reached out.

Don't be too disappointed if not much comes of your job fair experience. Sometimes in the chaos quality people don't get the call. Your Master Résumé may well not be the perfect fit for their company without the tailoring you would normally rely upon to make it perfect. If that's the case, and later you find a great role at that company, make it specific to that role and resubmit the résumé; it will be updated in their system.

Having gone over the different avenues for getting you the best route into that next great company, let's go over a set of rules to remember as you prepare to submit yourself.

25 Golden Rules of Résumé Submission

1. Quality Over Quantity—Always: A common myth out there relates to how many résumés you should circulate at one time. The belief is that thanks to the blessing of the Internet, one can send out tens, even **hundreds** of résumés at one time. It's called **résumé blasting.** It's **so** easy! Applicants fantasize that with such a volume assault; there simply **must** be any number of companies who will bite. The phone will likely be ringing off the hook with companies hoping to interview them. Perhaps a bidding war over their talent will result! If you have a slim chance with **one** company, surely having your résumé in front of a **hundred** companies increases your chances?

   Nonsense.

   Sending a flurry of submissions and spamming your résumé over job boards has numerous downsides that negate any possible increase that volume might otherwise provide:

- When applicants choose to go the volume route, they sacrifice the individual attention to each role, the detailed focus of the submission to the specific needs of each company. This alone takes away the power of a strong application and drags the résumé down from great to average.

- Having your résumé in front of so many sources dilutes your brand name in the marketplace. If you are special, are exceptional (and you **are** with your new résumé and cover letter), then you can be selective in your choices. In agencies multiple submissions to multiple roles from one applicant diminish their view of your worth. If you submit yourself to ABC Company for a Display Coordinator on Tuesday, then a Marketing Representative Friday, it does **not** double your chances, but rather risks your inclusion on a kind of recruiter blacklist. Remember, you're not **helping** them by doing this, you're wasting time with a shotgun instead of that laser.

- When your résumé is seen multiple times by a recruiter, it does not necessarily increase the chances that they will contact you. You can submit a limited number of focused résumés to the same company, but bulk generic send outs will be interpreted as desperation by a recruiter.

- When you send out multiple volume-based submissions, it becomes more and more difficult to keep track of them all. If you have phone screens set up with 3 companies and 1st interviews with 4 others, you will likely duplicate information with some recruiters and omit important facts from others. I've seen it time and again. The confusion and lack or perceived organization can be fatal to your job search.

- Recruitment agencies have little patience for the candidate who interviews at many agencies, has her résumé all over the job boards, and has already applied themselves to tens of companies through their web portals. They will avoid working with you not because you're not capable, but because you're common goods, accessible to everyone.

We will **not** be putting all our eggs in one professional basket, of course, and diversification of your submissions will absolutely help. What we want to avoid is the common mistaken belief that more is better.

2. Follow Their Rules. It's amazing. A website asks you to submit your résumé in doc format, with reference to the job number in your subject line. The research shows that 10–17% of applicants send it in either pdf format when told otherwise, or neglect to include the job number as requested…**why???** Perhaps the name of the recruiter is listed in the posting…use it and spell it correctly or else! One theme you will have noticed in this book is that one of the best ways to impress a recruiter is to make their job easier. Not only does ignoring the submission procedures that recruiters lay out inhibit their ability to review your information quickly and effectively, but it smacks of candidate flaws like lack of attention to detail and inability to follow simple instructions that may well disqualify you **immediately!**

One benefit of focusing on fewer, yet more high quality opportunities to begin your search is that you will place greater importance on them. As a result, you will take your time on each application, reading their rules for submission and sticking to them. You want this. Even if you do **nothing** else I have laid out in this book, following to the letter the application and submission instructions of a hopeful new employer will put you ahead of that 10–17% group of knuckleheads every time.

If my name is spelled incorrectly, the résumé will be discarded… this is an absolute no-no. It shows lack of respect and attention to detail.
Carla Perry—Sr. Recruiter, David Aplin Recruting.

3. Don't Bother with Snail Mail. This was an area where my research actually surprised me. While I personally have ambivalent feelings towards résumés sent through the postal service, I felt that there would still be a few traditionalists who appreciate the old school approach. I also believed that a percentage of recruiters might have their attention caught by a mailed résumé due to the sheer novelty of it; because it's just not **done** anymore. Shall I tell you how many of the **Résumé Success 600** would be attracted to a mailed résumé?

ZERO. Not a single one.

There was a transitional period after the heyday of stamped and mailed résumés wherein scanning résumés to add to a database was a part of the submission process. However, with the advent, popularity, and brilliance of current Applicant Tracking Systems to import information electronically, submission by regular mail has truly breathed its final breath. Not only is it common, but emailed or ATS populated résumés actually save the recruiter time. And you understand by now how precious little of it they have. Regular mail makes their work **harder,** so don't do it.

4. Keep a Job Search Journal. The format it takes is not important. Be it on your computer, or longhand on a writing tablet, you need to keep record of your applications from start to finish. As you get deeper into your search and the information multiplies, it becomes simply too challenging to keep it all straight, and it's easily remedied.

It will be necessarily efficient for you to be organized, saving you time digging for callback numbers and contact names as you juggle direct submissions, agency recruiters, job fair information, contacts, and the hundred other things required in your job search.

Equally important, though, is that having a clearly laid out order of operations and listing of who, where, what, when, and how so that you don't screw up! Countless times we recruiters come across an applicant who can't remember which résumé she sent to us, or which job he was applying to, or uses the wrong name while addressing our firm or us! People book interviews too close to each other, lose contact information, go to the wrong address, miss application deadlines, ignore follow up calls, all due to poor organization. It is **so** easy to disqualify these people! Why would great companies want to hire someone who can't keep such elementary information in order?

5. Never Pay to Get Your Résumé Anywhere. There exist a vast number of predatory businesses that take advantage of the anxiety

> *Definitely not snail mail, as I work hard to manage the amount of paper that crosses my desk, and I file résumés electronically. A hard copy delivery, therefore, adds work, as I need to scan it and file it, rather than simply downloading from an email.*
> Cheryl Malton— Communications and Recruitment Specialist, Smuckers Foods

and desperation of some job seekers and offering little in the way of value. The Internet is rife with 'services' that will get your résumé out to thousands of companies, multiplying your chances of getting that job by many times!!!

Poppycock. Not only are they breaking the rules of quality over quantity and all the diminished impact of your professional brand that résumé blasting results in, but also it just plain doesn't work. These companies often use software so closely resembling, and in some cases identical to, spamming programs, that your résumé will likely not make it past a company spam filter. Trust me, company spam filters are **very** good, and their mandate is not 'accept if we think this may be a résumé' but rather 'garbage because they've done something not in line with our process'. Heck, sometimes my emails to my corporate clients ended up caught in a spam filter just because I CC'd a couple of other colleagues or because my company logo is included in the message!

I have yet to find one of these résumé distribution companies that take the care and sincerity required for a genuine application. I also have yet to hear from one of my candidates who have used these services that resulted in being hired through them. Save your money.

6. Check, Check...Check...Click. The ease with which you can get your résumé or application to a company online commonly results in terrible mistakes being made that ruin your chances before you even have a foot in the door.

Email your résumé and cover letter to yourself first. Make sure that the subject line, saved file titles, and information is just as you intend and free of errors.

If your application to a company requires that you enter information into a number of fields in an online job portal, which is now regularly the case, make sure that you review every single entry before hitting **enter.** Some sites are not bug free and you refresh the screen and think you've lost something and start again when it's already been sent. Other sites don't allow you to go back to prior pages. Be careful! They likely won't have spell check on their application program, so if a lengthier answer is required, write it in Word, then cut and paste it into the box offered.

Whether you text from your pda or cellphone, respond via remote laptop, or compose on a home pc, you must commit to check **every** piece of communication to a recruiter for completeness, readability, and correctness. Just this morning I booted a candidate from a search because while I felt he was technically capable of the succeeding in the role, every single email to me had errors. Unprofessional and therefore not worth my client's time. Honest truth. Gone.

Wrest your mind from the new electronic mentality that anything can be undone. Imagine when you hit send or go to the next page that you're dropping that information in a stamped envelope into a mailbox…it's gone. Take your time and do it right.

7. Avoid Posting Publicly on Job Boards…at First. Job boards, as we've covered, are outstanding at making available a vast number of applicants to an immense number of companies. But you need to be careful that less-scrupled people don't use your information for less than savory purposes.

At the very minimum, many poor quality recruiters from agencies will just surf through résumé postings and scrape the information into their company Applicant Tracking System. This reduces your brand in that the formatting is usually very poor and your résumé is more general. Should you have been able to apply to a position represented by this agency directly, you would have been able to put together a top-notch submission. But now, without your knowledge, they have a diluted version of your professional worth in their files and if they do future searches you won't seem a strong fit.

Another, more significant reason for not publically posting your information is identity theft or improper solicitation. The value of the personal information you list on your résumé, from contact information to education, from employers to personal interests can be a magnet for illegal entities looking to exploit you or your name. It's not common…but it's less rare than you might think.

A good way around this is to post your résumé privately. On most sizeable boards you can select the option of keeping your personal information private, while allowing interested parties to view your professional qualifications and employment history. Should they be interested in you, they click a key and it sends you an email asking you to open the file to them. This option gives you the additional control that can keep you safe. It also whispers of exclusivity of your professional information that may show recruiters that only serious companies should contact you. This appeal will usually far outweigh the slight inconvenience of having that extra step involved in contacting you. I have never avoided contacting an otherwise well-qualified candidate because they posted their résumé privately. I was actually happy to get the email letting me know they'd 'approved' me!

> **Caveat:** You must make sure you **check often and release** your information when requested. If a recruiter or company asks for full disclosure and you wait several days, they've likely moved on to other candidates.

A great alternative to this method is to publically post, but when you find a set of quality agency recruiters to work for you, tell them that if they take you to market you will remove your résumé from that board for a period of time. This returns your brand to more exclusivity and they will appreciate the move. Make sure they keep you busy with quality interviews if you do this. This alternative is used when your first lines of attack haven't met with success. If your experience simply isn't up to it, the generic public posting of your résumé **can** work…

8. Don't Apply to Jobs that Aren't a Match. Start your search with only the most relevant and perfect fits as they relate to the job description. If you don't hit at least 66% or more of their needs, move on. Remember, **their** requirements, not yours. Focus your first and strongest efforts on the short list of your closest matches. They are your best bets.

Should these applications not result in the success you are expecting, then apply to those with 60% a fit, then 50%. I strongly urge that you do **not** apply to positions that you are less than 50% qualified for unless it is a junior role and the employer is weighting their preference heavily on one or two aspects you **do** already possess. It does you no favors, as there will absolutely be people better suited experientially for the role. You will have a brilliant résumé, but at some point you must recognize that the role you are considering is just not for you.

9. References are Always Available. It was stated earlier that you needn't make note of references on your résumé. That doesn't mean you don't need, them, however. They are a very important aspect of your overall application.

Recruiters check references for a couple of reasons: They may need to simply do their due diligence to check that you actually did work for that prior company when you said you did. This is a **fact-checking** refer-ence. When this kind of reference is done, they often have made up their mind to hire you and they just want to dot their i's and cross their t's. The other instance a recruiter will call a reference is a **quality-check.** They want to know what you did there, but in addition they want to know how well you did it. They want to know if you are great; if the company the ref-erence comes from loved you! This is an important distinction because this second kind of reference can land you the job. The company you applied to may be on the fence between you and another candidate, and sometimes the references can really make the difference!

For these reasons you must have references, and they must be good ones. Prepare a **minimum** of **two** professional and **one** personal refer-ences. The professional ones should ideally be with people to whom you directly reported, and at your most recent positions. If you have led people, it can pay to have one subordinate reference as well, so that the new employer can check that you led people well. The personal reference can be someone who has known you for at least 5 years and can speak about the kind of person you are; this is also called a **character reference.**

This may seem obvious, but make **certain** that they'll say great things about you!! Just as a quality reference can help you land that next job, a poor one can make sure it's snatched away. If given the option of using a very recent lukewarm reference or one slightly older but glowing, use the glowing one first.

Call your references and tell them that they will be contacted by your prospective employers. Have your list of references, with their company names, titles, phone numbers, and email addresses ready to give to your recruiter **before** they ask. Scrambling around at the 11th hour to get ahold of a reference who's out of country is a pain and unnecessary at the end of the recruitment process.

10. No Tricks. I hope I've given you the impression in this book that tricks are for amateurs and they run a greater risk of alienating a recruiter than endearing them to you. I meant it. No fancy paper, no bouquets, or special delivery letters.

I'm not saying such tactics never work, but they're too risky and you needn't bother.

This includes video and audio résumés. Several years ago these were seen to be the **next big thing** in application…but they didn't take, and now they're just another novelty that doesn't work. The insider secrets and advice in this book are **not** tricks. Rather, they are true and rarely shared tactics that flesh out your ideal strategy to legitimately get your résumé to the top of the pile.

11. The Job Search *IS* Your Job. If you want the next place you hang your vocational hat to be all you hope, you have to put work into it. Learning, building, and submitting your résumé are not easily done. Sorry, let me rephrase that. It's easy to do it poorly. It's less easy to do it **well.** It's downright challenging to do it brilliantly. That's why you bought this book. It takes time and effort, and it needs to be taken seriously. It's important to realize while you go through the steps to make your own résumé and take it to market there are hundreds, even thousands in your field, even in your area of expertise doing the same thing. You need to provide this process the attention needed to do it right. Half-hearted involvement in this will reap mediocre opportunities. You will be a 'B' or 'C' candidate and be sent to 'B' or 'C' positions at 'B' or 'C' companies.

If you are not working, consider **this** your job. Even if you are currently employed, think of this as a serious part-time role. You may envision that it's not a paying job, but it is! The effort you exert here will offer additional income and better prospects for your future. Picture it as both an education to supplement your qualifications, and also the negotiator in your pocket who will open doors to newfound money, fun, and professional opportunity previously closed to you.

You take your career seriously so you must take the process of creation and application equally seriously! I have seen it make a difference in more instances than I can count. If you really don't have the time to follow the steps in this book, hire a professional to create your résumé for you but never neglect to keep them honest and in line what you learn here. Your résumé is truly your most important professional document and deserves your time and respect.

12. Call in to the Company. Oooh, this one's going to get me in trouble. This is a real catch-22 subject. Recruiters want you to personalize your submission to them. They prefer you to have their name, to know if the job is still available, follow up, and so on. Most company websites are slow to update job availability, so it really does help to know if a position has already been closed. It's best to have the information but when you call in, you meet up with the reception gatekeeper who's job is to keep you from bothering people.

Companies have created a wall of anonymity to protect the valuable time of their recruiters, but it's resulted in a barrier against the same sincerity that they appreciate!

So call in. Be honest and let them guide you. If you have a number for Human Resources at the company call in and ask for the name of the person recruiting for the position you want to apply for, and if it's still open. If they ask why you want to talk to them, let them know you are interested in the posted role and you want to make sure you address it to the right recruiter. They will either give you the information, or tell you how you should address it generically.

If you need to start the process with the company switchboard, you can take one of two tacks: You can ask to speak with someone in HR. Either they will put you through or, more likely, ask you what you are calling about. When you tell them they'll either put you through or tell you to follow the online instructions or some similar standard answer designed to keep you from getting through to the poor recruiter struggling with their deadlines.

I have found that a great way to get past reception gatekeepers is to be honest; sincerely, earnestly, and in a detailed fashion. It gets them on your side and/or it eats their own valuable time. See, they have a lot of calls bottlenecking behind and around yours, and as you tell them about your process and your desire to make sure that the position is still open and that it gets to the right person because you're worried it may be lost because another time it got lost at another company and you're **perfect** for the role…they'll get tired and help you through. It's honest and it works.

Do what you can to get through and learn what you can to bring your submission to that next level. Don't, however, be discouraged if you can't get through, or are shut down at reception, or given the cold shoulder at any point in the process. It doesn't in any way affect their opinion of you or your application. Just try your best because it can't hurt and can certainly help. According to responses from the **Résumé Success 600** group, a résumé gets 'extra points' if they can address it to the right person (and spell their name right)!

If you don't get that information and you're wondering how to address your submission, 'Dear Recruiter' is perfectly acceptable. Do

Call or web search the organization to get the HR Manager or Recruiter's name if possible.

Cheryl Deneau— Recruitment Specialist, Chatham Kent Health Alliance

not address it; 'To Whom it May Concern'...the days of this cold, catch-all salutation are done. At least if you address it to a recruiter they will feel a mild sense of connection with it.

You can also use the same techniques to call in after to ensure that the recruiter received it. This is a little less well received, so be polite and brief. If the web portal application provides you with some form of indication that it has been successfully received or sends you an email confirming receipt, don't call.

13. Don't Talk Money...YET. Never ever include your salary expectations on your résumé and cover letter submission. Even if an online job board posting or application portal at a company site ask for it and have a nice, clean little dialog box to fill it in, don't do it. **Even** if they tell you it's a required field, fill in the others and see if you can get to the next section without filling it in. If it asks you for a range give a very wide range. Try entering a '.' and it may let you move to the next screen.

The reason is not to withhold information from a recruiter but because it's too early in the process to talk money. It's like meeting a cute member of the opposite sex and in your first conversation talking about a DJ for the wedding.

The reality is that they don't know enough about you yet to discount you due to salary. In many instances there can be flexibility in a posted salary range if the person is ideal. Even more important is that **you** haven't qualified the position enough to give a quality salary range for yourself. This next role may be ideal for you in every way, or you may know you were overpaid at your last employer, or you may want less stressful work, or any number of reasons why you may lower your own price point.

Recruiters find that many applicants have unreasonable expectations regarding what they are worth to a new employer. They overprice themselves and get left out of the process. It also happens that candidates were grossly underpaid in their prior role, and can command a higher price point. Get the interview first. Get a feel for each other and the positives and negatives of the position and company.

You may think that this is a vital piece of information and that you will not get a call to interview if you don't include it...not so. It **is** important to cover, but not just yet. I have **never** had a candidate who had a strong résumé kicked out of a process for not providing this information at the outset.

14. Use *ALL* Possible Sources. You will be very selective as you begin your search about which roles you will choose to apply for. This does not mean that you can go to one source such as a huge job board, find 5 winning postings, and hit those ones hard. Don't put all your Submission eggs in one basket. Visit other boards, company websites, access your recruiters, and even check out old-fashioned newspapers for roles as some companies still choose to advertise there.

If you rely upon one source and it has a flaw, such as a job board that does not update its listing frequently, your entire first effort could be for naught as you discover the linked roles are already filled! Diversification of your submission sources insures against this. It also gives you the reason to investigate multiple sources…who knows, you may find several **much** higher in quality than the one you first happened upon. It gives you a greater education about where to find roles and what each source expects, and success rates there. If you apply to three roles through the newspaper and hear nothing at all, but your agency recruiter lands you two interviews at her client companies, then you've learned something about where in the future you might want to focus more effort.

15. Don't Compromise…Until You Have to. It doesn't matter if you're fresh out of high school or are president of a multi-billion dollar corporation, your résumé will be of first-rate quality and you shouldn't sell yourself short. Submit yourself to the best roles first, have confidence in your ability to land a fantastic position. Don't cut corners, especially your own. Assume that your integrity, experience, and professional documentation will land you the job you want.

If time passes and your submissions are not having the traction you expect, you can expand your circle and apply to roles that aren't your ultimate fit, but still great. Hold out as long as you can for the perfect roles, but then expand your reach and relax your expectations a bit. There are many more 'B' quality roles out there than 'A's, and you can still find a great professional home at a 'B'. There will be many roles out there that represent a compromise for you, but an acceptable one.

If you come to a place where you are having no luck and are considering scraping the bottom of the barrel and hooking up with a lowly 'C' quality role, talk to a professional recruiter for feedback, and only use it as a stopgap. It may be that you lack the background at present to land a higher quality role.

Your résumé can illuminate the areas you need to develop in order to qualify for the next rung up the ladder. There may be habitual, experiential, communication, or education based challenges that you can overcome over time so that the following role steps you up into a 'B' or even an 'A' company and position!

16. Improve Your Candidacy. If you are being selective about where you work next it may take you time to find the right role. During that time you should do all within your power to improve your qualifications for the roles you are seeking to land, and then let people know about it.

If you have found in your research that you seem to have many of the qualities your target companies are looking for, but you lack an important ingredient, take care of it! Take a course if you need to become better qualified or work towards a designation. Some employers won't require that you **have** the designation so long as you are along the way to getting it and commit to completion.

Perhaps there is an area of responsibility that most quality employers are looking for that you lack that you identified in Chapter 2. If you are currently unemployed, take a course, attend a seminar, get tutored by an expert, or study online. If you are still working, ask for that responsibility in addition to your existing ones, or ask a colleague who has that skill set to allow you to assist. If it means less work for them after you're up to speed, they will likely agree.

17. The Closer the Match the Better the Catch. Starting with your strong Master Résumé, it will **always** be your goal to craft a Focus Résumé for each and every quality position. The closer your application is to what they like and expect the greater your chances of being called. Period. Here are some tips to remember to ensure you are doing everything possible to relate:

- Get the recruiter's name and address it to them

- Have the job posting number and exact title and use them

- Go to the company website and read it thoroughly, looking for the type of personality and qualities they possess and want in their employees, and make sure your résumé and cover letter contains these

- Use the job description to find keywords that you will make sure are contained liberally in your résumé and cover letter, increasing the hit rating of your submission

- If you know anyone, even if you just spoke with reception and got a name, use it. Name-dropping works

- Use the job description to identify areas of your experience or education to highlight. If they are looking for someone with small company experience, make sure you emphasize this. If they want someone who can create macros in MS Excel, then don't just list that you know Excel, highlight your expertise!

18. Don't Take it Personally. Sometimes people won't call you back. Sometimes you will send off what you believe to be the best submission the world has ever seen...and nada...nothing. You call, email, and yell and the world seems to have fallen silent. Don't take it to heart.

Understand that you can only control **one** side of this affair. Your résumé and cover letter may really be the best! But perhaps they've already filled the role, or have to wade through the first hundred résumés before they start on the pile you're in. Maybe the recruiter has gone off sick or on maternity leave and the replacement hasn't yet been found or isn't yet up to speed. It happens that the hiring manager or senior executives put a position on hold, or pull the plug entirely.

There is a myriad of things that can result in lack of contact once your submission is in. **None** of these are your fault and there's little you can do but be patient and do your best to keep in touch.

19. Even if a Top Company has No Job for You...Apply. You may be looking for your ultimate job right now, but the timing may not be perfect yet. Say, for example, you identify three companies within a reasonable commute from your home that are listed in the 'Top 100 Companies to Work For'. These are **all 'A'** quality companies, so you go to their website but while you know they have positions like yours in existence, none are vacant now....submit anyway!

You never know when opportunity will knock. Say in a month or two years they have need of someone **just like you**...what's the first thing they'll do after evaluating whether or not an internal employee wants the job? **Check their Applicant Tracking System!** If you have proactively contacted them, submitted a Master Résumé tweaked to fit their corporate culture or better yet a Focus Résumé based upon all you know about a role at that company and update it whenever you can, rife with job-specific keywords, they will do a search and find you!

Also, a great proactive choice is to visit the career section of the company site, and if there's nothing there for you, you can create that Job Alert so that you can be at the front of the line when something comes up!

Don't rely exclusively on this method, however, as some companies don't utilize their ATS to its fullest, and when a relevant role comes up they may not have your résumé saved correctly, or enter search parameters that don't allow the system to 'find' you. It's best to submit yourself but remain vigilant.

20. Follow the Proper Order of Operations. Recruiters like myself are often mystified when a candidate contacts us about a posted position but is not prepared to interview, or has no résumé in hand. Or perhaps they are ready to go to interview my client company but know little about them. Maybe they are heading into **final** interviews and don't even have their references lined up. It also happens that it's Friday afternoon and they are supposed to start at their dream job with my client on Monday…and they haven't even quit their present job. There is a general order for submission that you might want to use so that you don't get caught in such an embarrassing situation: one that could cost you the role.

21. Don't Stop Until You've Got a Signed Offer Letter! Recruiters will encourage you to stop all other job search activity when you're interviewing with their clients, especially if you've passed the first interview and are awaiting a possible final interview or offer. They will be out of luck and out of pocket if you reach the end of their process and ultimately sign with another company.

As much as we hate this as recruiters, you **must** continue to feed the pipeline of your job search possibilities until you have a signed offer letter and a start date with a new company. For every instance where a candidate has jumped ship and taken another offer at the 11th hour, there is a client who had promised an offer to a candidate that didn't materialize in the end.

As your great résumé leads to interviews, remain active in your job search. Continue to put great effort into identifying brilliant companies and positions to apply to. Be enthusiastic about the prospect of getting an offer, but don't count on it. If it falls through, you have other irons in the fire and can just change your direction instead of having to ramp up the whole process again.

Be honest with the recruiters about your activities. You needn't tell them what companies you've applied to, but if you've been interviewed, and especially if you've been for a 2nd interview, they should know. They may not love that you are interviewing elsewhere, but they **will** respect it, and it won't hurt your candidacy at all. In fact, knowing that you are a bit in demand may actually help speed up the process and/or assist in your negotiations.

22. Stick 2 Gr8 Communication Etiquette. When you communicate email with a recruiter, never use shortcuts. Text-speak may be becoming more and more common, but it's never appropriate in business communication.

Also, address every email with the appropriate salutation. Many people are neglecting the usual 'Hello David' used to introduce what will follow, and start right in with the content. Avoid this, even if the recruiter chooses this form. You needn't use *'Dear…'*, as email has evolved into a form much different from the traditional letter, but a salutation is proper etiquette.

23. Send Your Résumé to at Least One Colleague. While the need for a second set of eyes to evaluate and edit your résumé content has already been emphasized, format checking is another important reason to send your résumé to a friend prior to submission.

There are different versions of Word, different operating systems, different screen types and sizes, and they can all contribute to inconsistent results as a recruiter opens your résumé. If you've worked diligently at condensing your résumé to two pages with some creative margin alterations, it may be that a recruiter will open it up and it will dribble onto that third page. It may appear clearly on their computer, but when printed out splay over multiple pages, or display odd gaps or altered fonts. The gremlins that plague multiple computing formats and systems are not yet banished from our world, and so we must be careful.

Send your résumé to a colleague and ask them if it opened as it should. Have them print it on their own printer and ensure that it looks as professional as you intended. While this will not guarantee that there will be no issue in your official submission, it can go a great way to ensuring your application remains error free.

24. Be Reachable. Recruiters love applicants who are accessible. When their attention turns to you and your résumé, they want instant access. If they send you an email or pick up the phone to call, you need to make sure that even if you're not at the other end of the line, they know you'll reply or return the call asap. Every minute counts in their day, and you don't want them forgetting you or passing you by just because you have no Internet access or didn't get a phone message!

While you search, you must be able to check your email often to reply to recruiters. If you are currently working and cannot do so, make it a priority to check before work and as soon as you get home…and once more before bed and on the weekends. Always reply quickly, and if they ask for a résumé and you don't have it where you are, send a note anyway, letting them know you received their email and will forward it to you that evening. Keep them connected to you.

A peeve of many recruiters involves phone contact. We've covered the importance of a direct phone number, but this issue comes up so often it needs to be emphasized again. If it's your cell phone number you listed on the résumé, check for messages often and call back as soon as possible. Recruiters will understand that you are busy, but won't want to wait a day for a call back. Avoid answering the call if you're in an awkward situation. The recruiter will leave a message with their contact number. Call back when you can give them your full attention…but **soon.**

Make sure your voicemail message greeting is clear, polite, and represents your best communication! If a recruiter can hardly make out what you're saying, or hears your theme music pounding in the background, or is offended with the tone of your greeting…they may well just hang up and move on!

INSIDER SECRET

If it's your home phone number you leave and you are out, let anyone who may answer the phone know that they may be getting calls from recruiters. They should know how to get in contact with you and/or you should be checking in for messages often.

If you are currently working you should only leave your business number if you want to get calls at the office. If a recruiter calls, can you take the call discretely? You don't want to seem to be blowing off an interested recruiter if you have your boss in front of you!

You **must** be available for recruiters to contact, and you must reply as soon as humanly possible. Even if it's a quick call or note to let them know you received their message and will reply in full that evening, it keeps you connected and the momentum flowing. You don't want to give them a reason to file your résumé and move on to someone else.

25. Always Keep Your Résumé Up-to-Date. Regardless of your employment circumstances, you must be forever vigilant in updating your résumé. As you update your qualifications and improve your fit for the best jobs, don't be shy about letting people know about it! Call your recruiters, update your résumé, and send the new version to companies who have your résumé on file with an addendum at the end of your cover letter explaining your update. Any improvement helps, and also acts as an easy and relevant reason to be in contact with the recruitment source. It can only help, and your most recent version will be saved in their ATS and your new qualifications will be searchable next time they check.

Of course, should you be unemployed, it stands to reason that you are prepared with an excellent document in hand. If you are working now at any level, however, and feel safe with your work situation, things can change very quickly.

When they do, you need to be ready.

While at times a savvy employee can see the writing on the wall and anticipate a pending company 'purge', most often it comes as a surprise. A reorganization, a restructuring, a relocating of offices, a realignment, a merger or acquisition, they are all now a common reality of working in corporate North America, and they most often represent a significant redundancy of great employees like yourself. When you want to move on, need to move on, or are moved on against your will, you will be ready for that bold next step if you have your résumé already prepared.

Picture this: you are told that your entire department is to be moved out of country and that your services, regrettably, will no longer be required. Your colleagues begin to scramble, dusting off old résumés or cobbling together new ones using their prior, and largely outdated information. They must grind their minds into action, mentally preparing for submissions, interviews, and marketing their skills to prospective new employers. It's a very stressful time, and their lack of preparedness is reflected in the false starts they suffer before having any traction with their job hunt.

You, on the other hand, while having enjoyed your experience with this company, have always kept your Master Résumé updated just in case your situation changed. Should a headhunter have pursued you with an outstanding new opportunity, or should the need to commence a new search yourself arise, you needed only tailor your résumé to each new possibility. The anxiety, uncertainty, and insecurity associated with a job hunt have already been reduced; you've been prepared. You get out of the gates earlier, are more in tune with your skills, abilities, and experiences, having revisited them often, and will more likely be identified as an 'A' candidate and transitioned to a newer, perhaps much better role quickly and easily.

Here are some key tips to keep your Master Résumé sharp:

- Update it every 6 months no matter what your employment situation
- Create and keep a Résumé File containing a copy of your most recent version, so that in between updates you can revisit it, adding:
  - Performance appraisals
  - Commendations or recognition
  - New job descriptions
  - Important new company information (e.g. now #1 in marketplace)
  - Any accomplishments you may want to add to your next résumé
  - Details of any training, workshops, certifications, presentations if they are relevant and worthy
  - New responsibilities added
- You may want to save the new file with a year date, such as **'davidjgardner_sales_resume_2013.doc'**, so that if in the future you choose a direction that reflects experiences from earlier in your career, you can readily access that Master Résumé version

Your résumé should always be up to date even if you are not actively looking for new opportunities. There is nothing more frustrating than looking at a résumé that is not current. If you tell a recruiter you have not had a chance to update your résumé…you are not ready!
Jennifer Knight—
Compass Group Canada

Now you have a firm grasp of the details recruiters look for in an excellent résumé, you can save them along the way, and have them on hand for subsequent updates. When it comes time to review the file, you will have all the relevant evidence of your ongoing development to add that will bring your résumé to even greater heights.

Submission of your résumé represents the last of the 5 Master Keys to Résumé Success. You've likely been surprised by the many tactics and approaches needed to have immense success as you get your professional documentation out and into the marketplace.

As with any of the other Master Keys, you can ignore the steps and take the simplest, easiest, and quickest avenue…but that road is crowded with a multitude of also-rans clamoring to every open door. Yours must be a cut above. As master of this key you will knock on doors closed to others and find recruiters opening them for you with a smile.

Chapter 8 Summary

- The most effective résumés are Focus Résumés tailored to a specific role

- You may choose to submit your résumé to a selected company recruiters AND/OR agency recruiters:
    - Without a posted role to be added to their current Applicant Tracking System
    - To a listed role to be considered for it expressly

- Approach 7–10 recruitment agencies and meet them to evaluate whether you can work together

- The Phone Screen can be used by a recruiter to evaluate your communication and experience; take it seriously or risk missing a face-to-face meeting

- Become an 'A' candidate and agency recruiters will work diligently and loyally on your behalf

- Ask questions in interview with agency recruiters to evaluate if they're serious and qualified to help you

- Job Boards can grant you access to a high number of relevant jobs quickly

- Job Alert programs at Job Boards or company sites will automatically email you when a closely-matching role becomes available

- Networking helps for referrals, but it is a lengthy and ongoing process

- Job Fairs are useful places to submit résumés, view valuable presentations, and learn more about companies you may want to join; make sure you go prepared and follow up professionally

- 25 Golden Rules of Submission

Chapter STEPS

STEP 6a: Create a Focus Résumé document file

Since the most effective résumé is an accurate reflection of you as an employee, continual, relevant, conscientious professional improvement will only make future résumés that much more powerful.

Barrie Carlyle
—Director, Knightsbridge
Human Capital Solutions

chapter 9

Conclusion and Beyond!

Well That's It!

As we wrap up and have you move on to getting your résumé out there and in to the welcoming hands of recruiters frustrated with the traditional refuse, I want you to know that I have tremendous respect for you. Taking this most important part of your career seriously to such a high degree is something so very few do, and recruiter recycle bins are overflowing with the evidence. I have seen countless people, even people really who know better, take shortcuts and compromises that saved time and effort and resulted in an impotent résumé.

If you have paid attention and followed the rules laid out, the guidelines listed, the processes explained, your résumé is, as promised, in the top 5% of **all** résumés in your market space. As you send it out you will likely discover surprising opportunities opening up to you. As you are propelled towards your next great career move and beyond, take credit for yourself and this document...you've earned it.

If you have completed this book and do not yet have in your hand a proud Master Résumé and template, cover letter, and even Focus Résumé if you've identified a specific role, then please read through the chapters, sections, and steps again as you've likely missed something.

It's important to pay attention to every secret, highlight, quote, and step in the process to bring you to the very top of your presentation.

If you have any questions, don't hesitate to reach out to me. By buying this book we've become partners in your career success. You can reach me at **david@davidjgardner.com**.

It's important that you have confidence in your new professional image! If a recruiter suggests any changes to your résumé, consider them very carefully. They **may** have insight into your particular industry and appropriate presentation . . . but it's possible that they're just giving you their **personal** preference and they're wrong. Remember that the insights of over 600 years of recruiting from top agencies and businesses reviewing more than 7 million résumés are on **your** side.

Prepare for greatness!

Success in Your Next Job: Experience Revisited

In creating your Master Résumé, and the Focus Résumés you will build for each qualified role, we've relied upon using the experience you bring to the table. We've worked diligently to take what may have been ordinary experience and made it extraordinary.

This point challenged me, however . . . the Résumé Success principles can, once applied, cause great improvements in the understanding and perception of any work experience. In the end, however, the **ultimate** résumés, the very, very best, combine all that I teach with a **strong set of past experiences.** This allows a job hunter to reach the incredible top 1–2% in attractiveness to recruiters.

What if you had this extraordinary experience to **begin** with? Can you imagine how much more powerful your résumé would be if, in your previous roles you were an absolute hero?

- References would be a dream as your superiors would not only have recognized your talent, but be anxious to tell others about your many contributions

- You would command a higher price-point in your marketplace and be in demand regardless of how the economy is doing

- Others would look to you as the go-to person in your office

- Your career arc would increase its upward tick, avoiding plateaus and stagnation

- Management would be eager to groom you for promotions

In short, you would be able to write your own ticket.

I've met professionals like this, and talked to them about what gives them the edge over their peers. In fact, it's why I've risen to management in three completely different industries in a fraction of the time it took others in my field.

Was it intelligence? No.

Was it industry experience? No.

Was it education? No.

Here is some advice on how to make your next, and every subsequent role you have in the future a success.

1: Learn What is Expected of You

You would be surprised at how simple this concept is, and yet so rarely followed. Management at whatever level should have laid out for you what your role is at the company from the outset. Oftentimes more junior roles have specific responsibilities and it's easy to follow them. If you have this role-specific list of responsibilities, make that your starting point.

More senior roles rarely have such specific tasks laid out. In such cases you must be in touch with every relevant executive player in your company and ask them what they expect of you. Most people don't ask, and doing so it keeps both sides on the same page.

The manager or executive to whom you report will be glad you take interest in mastering the requirements of your role, and you should find them a willing ally.

Poorly-defined expectations readily leads to anxiety, frustration, and disappointment.

2: Master That!

If you have a list provided by your manager, follow it. If 'x' is a part of your job and yet your peers don't seem to be doing it…take the initiative and do it. Your goal here is to be sat down at your performance review and not have a single 'needs improvement'. If you take valuable time and effort to work on tasks that are not deemed important by management before you have the basics mastered, you run the risk of disappointing your leaders.

Remember Maslow's Stages of Competence? You want to develop yourself to the point where you rest in the **unconscious competent** level for your role.

Senior management must do the same. If you know the expectations of your role, the basics required to satisfy your boss; **start there.** Don't get ahead of yourself.

Use every piece of feedback to improve. Your clients, your colleagues, your management, will all contribute to help you advance your development.

Be careful, however, as some may have their own interests at heart. Also, some colleagues may have instituted a culture of 'just getting by'…this is not the route you want to take.

Do you have a manual or book that lays out what is required of you in your role? Read it, learn it, do it.

3: Learn What it Takes to be Outstanding and Continually Work Towards it!

After having proven that you understand your role and can readily fulfill expectations, your next step is to improve on them. You will likely have discovered by now who excels in your company and in what ways. Find out what is required to reach 'Exceeds Expectations' across the board on your performance reviews. The more you speak with your own boss the more you will learn what is important for that next step, from good to great.

Create a plan. Model a successful peer. Meet with your boss and ask for their help. Steady, incremental improvements over time will do wonders for your career. If you sold **'x'** last month, plan for **'x + y'** next month. If you are an accountant and month end takes 6 days, find a way to do it in 5. If you're in sales and last month you made 50 calls, do 60! You can copy the success of a peer, but then make it your own. Remember, doing more doesn't always mean spend more time at the office. Work smarter. Remember the Accomplishments section of your résumé? Work on those areas. Increase sales, beat a deadline, or take on additional responsibilities.

The above three successive steps appear condescendingly simple. I understand! I have interacted with, led, followed, interviewed, screened, and promoted innumerable people and have always paid attention to who got ahead and who fell behind. It's always been a habit of mine to see what was working for others professionally and invariably successful employees of every stripe followed these steps.

It doesn't end there…while the above steps represent the overall strategy for developing stronger and stronger résumés throughout your career, there are other ingredients that contribute.

Attributes of a Successful Professional

Success is more consistent than you think. These are some of the most consistent attributes of successful professionals:

Attitude—We constantly affect the people around us with our attitude. If you are positive and earnest in your work, not only will it buoy the people around you, management will take notice. You make the group better just be being there. Clients, peers, management, they all notice and appreciate a great attitude.

Passion—If you like what you do, and you should, at least, **like** what you do…even **love** what you do; show it! In interview and in day-to-day work life, someone who is passionate about their role, industry, company, team, division, leaders, and customers go further. People will always silently question your 'buy in'…do you really believe in what you're doing? If you do and people see it, they'll be on your side and buy more, help more, mentor more, and promote you more.

Goal-oriented—Management at every level loves the employee who sets higher standards and moves toward them. The very concept of setting goals implies that one is always striving to be better, to move themself and their company further ahead. Even if your role seems repetitive and mundane, no one wants a simple automaton. Show others that you continually improve, that you're a bright and ambitious work in progress, and doors will open for you.

Grooming—This may seem such a simple thing, and superficial, but your appearance has been proven to have a significant correlation to the opportunities that will manifest in a career. Better opportunities result in better experiences, and finally of course, in stronger résumés. Personal grooming habits like shaving, dental hygiene, appropriate haircut, and cleanliness, combined with professional dress, presents a successful package that management notices. Remember, management is always evaluating you. 'Is this person promotable?', 'Can I put this person in front of **my** boss?'; 'Does this person effectively reflect the face of our organization?'. If you are always groomed for success, their answers will be a resounding 'yes!' every day…and your career will never be impeded.

Clean and organized work area—Not only does a neat, tidy, and efficient work area reduce worker stress and help your productivity, senior brass love it. You rarely see a senior executive drowning in messy paperwork, files, documents, and assorted bric-a-brac strewn around their office. They take pride in their area, they work more effectively when its organized, and they expect their people to, as well. If you take the time and effort to emulate their commitment to efficiency and professionalism, you will do better, and they will notice.

If the BOSS were here, what would he/she say/do?—Whenever you are unsure about what to do in a situation at work, a **great** question to ask yourself is 'What would my boss do or say about this?' The answer to this question will cause you to become more aligned with management and corporate values. If you wonder if it would be fine to take an extra 30 minutes for lunch, ask what your boss would say. If the answer is no, then don't do it. If you are considering doing some research into ways to save your company money, ask yourself if your manager would approve. If yes, then do it. This can act as a fantastic professional barometer for your daily actions and decisions.

Meet deadlines—Another highly important judgment tool for management is whether or not an employee can meet or beat a deadline. Regardless of industry, the working world progresses according to timelines, and if we fail to adhere to them, the system cannot hold together. To you it may seem like one small thing, but the backlog behind that delay, and the loss of confidence that can result is too high a price to pay. Meet deadlines consistently and you will be recognized for it.

Takes on additional responsibility—Once you have mastered your own role, a useful tactic to move beyond into being identified as exceptional is to take on additional responsibilities. Mentor new employees, lead the recycling effort, plan an event, create a new manual for your area, improve a process...there is no limit to the number of additional responsibilities that you can take on to show management that you not only are capable of more then your existing role (promotable), but also care enough to put in the extra effort (good corporate ambassador). **Don't just take on extra work**...this can leave you exhausted, accomplishing less in your real focus area, and may be overlooked by your boss. Go to them when you know you are doing well with your regular role, and tell them you would very much like to take on a bit more responsibility. Extra responsibility may require more time and effort, but not necessarily. They'll love it...and you!

Think big picture—In any organization, but especially in large corporations, it's very easy to feel like a tiny cog in a huge machine. Workers are tagged and put in their little cubby holes, siloed and niched. It's important to think beyond your one role and to the company as a whole. How do you fit in? How can you contribute more to the overall apparatus? Asking your management questions about such things will show them that you're thinking big picture, and beyond your current role. Always succession planning, attempting to plan for future moves, they will appreciate your initiative.

Always take care of your clients—We **all** have clients. If you're in sales it's your customers, of course. But even if you don't feel you serve a customer base, your peers, your manager, your team...these are all people to whom you are accountable in serving their interests. If you're an associate professor, not only are your students your customers, so also are your Dean and faculty. Determine who your clients are and make sure you take good care of them.

Have integrity—Some professions, such as lawyers, doctors, and teachers, carry with them the hopeful assumption of integrity. Yet every role in every company or organization benefits from workers with integrity. If you know your role and unflaggingly carry it out without shortcuts or compromises, not only will you be a better employee, your management will notice.

Model greatness—Mentioned earlier, this is worth reemphasizing. Rather than reinventing the wheel to become a hero in your organization, find the person or people who are already great and emulate them. Modeling the attitudes, actions, and professional attributes of successful people will not only boost your career, you may find willing mentors and long-term friendships along the way.

Learn—Always learn. Read books, take courses, join associations or groups connected to your profession…self development for a professional in any area cannot possibly be emphasized enough. It makes the different between the exceptional and the ordinary. Avoid stagnation in your industry by continually updating your skills and information. Learn, learn, and learn.

This is of course an incomplete list. Taking the time to consider and develop these areas will, however, assist you in moving towards professional success and experience invaluable in your future résumés. It is designed to plant seeds in your mind of professional advancement such that you will later find other areas in which to focus and improve. Once you move in the direction these require you will discover your own new additions, relevant to your specific professional situation. Commit to following these steps and adopting these traits and it's virtually impossible to fail.

Share Your Success

I've promised to be as brief as possible but provide you with every-thing I, along with the rest of the **Résumé Success 600 Year Insider Team** have to offer in real, honest, no-bull résumé strategy. I hope it's been proven that it takes work, but that a résumé in the top 5% is achievable by anyone, regardless of background or industry, tenure or professional rank. If you work in a niche field and believe that some slight augmentation of the Master Résumé is needed for your area specifically, contact me and I'll do what I can to help.

As you find your next great position with your new résumé, I'd be thrilled to hear about your experience! Please send me an email at david@davidjgardner.com and let me know how *Résumé Success: Insider Secrets to Building the Résumé Top Companies Love!* helped you land that great new role.

Good luck my friend, and good hunting!

Index

CPSIA information can be obtained at www.ICGtesting.com
Printed in the USA
237392LV00005B/38/P